the Beginners' CHOICE

Workbook

Scott Thornbury

Pearson Education Limited,
Edinburgh Gate, Harlow,
Essex CM20 2JE, England

© Longman Group UK Limited 1992
All rights reserved; no part of this publication may be reproduced, stored in a retrieval system, or transmitted in any form or by any means, electronic, mechanical, photocopying, recording or otherwise, without the prior written permission of the Publishers.

First published 1992
Seventh impression 1999

Set in Adobe ITC Garamond Light and Frutiger
Printed in Malaysia, PJB

British Library Cataloguing in Publication Data
Thombury, Scott
The Beginners' Choice
Workbook
I. Title
428

ISBN 0 582 071003

Contents

Unit 0	4
Unit 1	6
Unit 2	9
Unit 3	12
Unit 4	15
Unit 5	18
Unit 6	20
Unit 7	23
Unit 8	26
Unit 9	29
Unit 10	32
Unit 11	34
Unit 12	37
Unit 13	40
Unit 14	43
Unit 15	46
Unit 16	49
Unit 17	52
Unit 18	55
Unit 19	58
Unit 20	61
Vocabulary building	64
Grammar review	66
Irregular verbs	71
Tapescript	72

Unit 0

1 Vocabulary =kelime bilgisi

Complete the crossword.

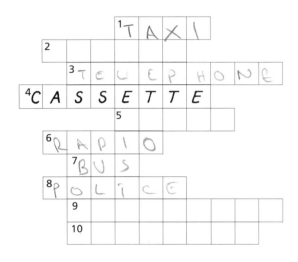

Down
1

Across = karşısında

2 Dictionary work

Use a dictionary. Translate the words into your language.

Verbs		**Nouns**	
	fiiller		isimler
read	Okumak	question	Soru
listen	dinlemek	answer	cevap
write	Yazmak	word	kelimeler
know	Bilmek	punctuation	Noktalama
spell	hecelemek	sentence	Cümle
complete	tamamlamak	text	metin
underline	altını çizmek	conversation	Konuşma
correct	doğru		
translate	Çevirmek		
match	kibrit		
order	emir		
list	Liste		
repeat	tekrarlamak		

3 Listening

Listen to the cassette. Write the words.

1 *video*
2 _____
3 _____
4 _____
5 _____
6 _____
7 _____
8 _____
9 _____

4 Pronunciation

Listen to the cassette and repeat the words.

5 Reading

Underline the words you know in the text.

Using your dictionary

This dictionary tells you a lot about English words and how to use them – in writing and speaking English, as well as in reading. Like any dictionary, it tells you the meaning of words and how to spell them, but it can also help you with word-building, grammar, pronunciation, and other important parts of the language.

Unit 1

1 Vocabulary

Put the letters in the correct order to make words about food and drink.

1 grasu
   sugar
2 klim
   _____
3 creela
   _____
4 feefoc or ate
   _____
5 stoat and darmamela
   _____
6 derab and tubert
   _____
7 sgeg and canob
   _____

2 Grammar: a/an; adjectives

Correct the mistakes.

1 an apple small
   a small apple
2 six chocolates hot
   six hot cholates
3 a egg
   an egg
4 a oranges juice
   _____
5 two coffees white
   two white coffees
6 an croissant
   a croissant
7 three black tea
   Three tea back
8 a English breakfast
   a breakfast English
9 three potatoes bigs
   three bigs potatoes

3 Reading

1 Read the text, and underline the names of food and drink.

The English Breakfast

Breakfast is the first meal of the day. It typically starts with a bowl of cereal with milk or cream, followed by toast and jam, marmalade or honey. This is accompanied by a cup of tea or coffee, usually with milk and sugar. The traditional breakfast also includes eggs, usually fried, with bacon or sausages. A healthy breakfast consists of orange juice, for example, then muesli or yoghurt, followed by a cup of decaffeinated coffee with milk but no sugar.

2 Read the text above and look at the pictures a, b and c. Now read the questions and underline the correct answer.

1 Which is the typical breakfast?   a b (c)
2 Which is the traditional breakfast? (a) b c
3 Which is the healthy breakfast?   a (b) c

a

b

c

4 Conversation — konuşma

Bu konuşmaları sırayla yazı — sıralama
Put these conversations in order. emir

1. No, thank you.
   Coffee?

   Coffee?
   No, thank you.

2. 2 Tea, please.
   1 Good morning, madam.
   3 Coffee or tea?
   2 Good morning. Breakfast, please.

   Good morning madam
   Good morning Breakfast please
   Coffee or tea
   Tea Please

3. Anything else? Başka birşey—
   Two eggs, please. 2· Yumurta Lütfen
   No, thank you. That's all. bu kadar.

   Two eggs please
   Anything else?
   No thank you That's all

4. With milk? sütlü
   1 Tea or coffee? Kahve
   3 Sugar? şeker
   2 Coffee, please. Kahve lütfen
   6 Yes, please. Evet lütfen
   4 No, no sugar, thanks. Hayır şeker Teş

   Tea or coffee
   Coffee please
   Sugar?
   No, no sugar, thanks
   With milk?
   Yes, please.

5 Listening

🎧 **Listen to the cassette and take the order.**

• CITY HOTEL •
Breakfast order

Room number: _____   Breakfast for _____ persons

6 Speaking

🎧 **Listen to the cassette and repeat.**

7 Numbers

Write the numbers.

1. eight five one three nine zero
   851390

2. five plus one is six
   5 + 1 = 6

3. two plus seven is nine
   2 + 7 = 9

4. three times two is six
   3 × 2 = 6

5. nine minus eight is one
   9 − 8 = 1

6. nine divided by three is three
   9 ÷ 3 = 3

7. nine five one zero three six two
   95 10 36 2

8. eight double five nine two four
   88 59 24

8 Listening

Listen to the cassette and write the numbers.

a _0223_
b _____
c _____
d _____
e _____
f _____
g _____
h _____
i _____
j _____

9 Grammar: Present Simple =Genişzaman

Write the questions for these answers.

1 _What do you have for breakfast?_
   Coffee and a <u>croissant</u>.
2 _____?
   Paolo.
3 _____?
   Italy.
4 _____?
   I–T–A–L–Y.
5 _____?
   987 641
6 _____?
   01039.

10 Pronunciation: word stress

Mark the stress on these words.

1 America
2 Norway
3 Italy
4 Australia
5 England
6 Canada
7 Japan
8 Brazil
9 Portugal

11 Writing

Punctuate the sentences.

1 shes in hong kong
   She's in Hong Kong.
2 its the hilton hotel
   it's the Hilton Hotel
3 im mark andrews
   my name is mark andrexxs
4 hes a waiter
   He is a waiter
5 youre a student
   You are a student
6 is this an english breakfast
   this is an english breakfast
7 do you have coffee with milk
   do you have with milk coffee
8 how many sugars do you have
   do you have how many sugars

Unit 2

1 Vocabulary: time   kelime bilgisi

1 Draw the clocks.

1 six o'clock   3 eleven forty-five   5 twelve o'clock

2 eight fifteen   4 ten thirty   6 eight forty-five

2 Vocabulary: places   kelime bilgisi yer

→Doğru   →yanlış

1 Read the sentences and write True or False.

1 You go to a cinema for a beer. __False__
2 You buy books in a bookshop. __True__
3 You go to a pub for a map. __False__
4 You go to a Tourist Information Centre for a cheque book. ____
5 You go to a cinema to see a film. __True__
6 You go to a café for stamps. ____
7 You go to a hotel for a room. __True__
8 You go to a pub for a beer. __False__
9 You go to a bank for a coffee. ____
10 You go to a bookshop for a cheque book. ____
11 You go to a Tourist Information Centre for a map. ____
12 You go to a post office to buy airmail letters. ____

2 Use some of the words in the exercise above to complete this telephone conversation.

Good morning. Is that Tourist Information? I want to cash a cheque: what time are the **banks** open? Thank you. And I want to see a _____: are cinemas open on Sunday? Good. Oh yes. I want a stamp: where is the _____? And one more question: when are the _____ open? I want a _____. Thank you very much. Goodbye.

3 Grammar: to be

Complete the sentences with am, is or are.

1 The banks _are_ open.
2 Etsuko _is_ at home.
3 Sorry, we _are_ closed.
4 Aisha and Sammy _____ English.
5 I _am_ a student.
6 The post office _are_ closed.
7 José-Ramon _is_ a teacher.
8 She _is_ at school.
9 It _is_ 9.30 and you _____ late!

4 Listening

Listen to the cassette and complete the information.

In Ireland shops are open from _nine_ to _____ , and _____ are open from 9.30 am to _____ Monday to Friday and they open again from _____ to 3.00. Shops are open on _____ but banks are closed on Saturdays and _____. Cinemas are open from _____ to _____, and pubs are open from 11.00 am to _____ every day except _____ when they close at _____.

5 Grammar: prepositions

Write complete sentences.

1 Australia/shops/9.00 am/5.30 pm
In Australia shops are open from 9.00 am to 5.30 pm.
2 Italy/banks/open/8.30 am/1.30 pm
in italy shops are open from
3 Milan/offices/open/8.00 am/2.30 pm
in milan offices open
4 Italy/shops/closed/1.00 pm/4.30 pm
in italy shops open closed
5 Rome/post offices/open/Saturday/8.00 am/2.00 pm
6 Italy/museums/closed/Monday

6 Speaking

Listen to the cassette and respond.

Example:
CASSETTE: bottle of milk
YOU: Can I have a bottle of milk, please?

7 Writing

At 3 I go back to the bank. I get to the bank at 9.00 am. On Friday I usually go to the cinema in the evening. I go home at about 6. My name is Montse. I usually go to the bank at 8. I get home at 6.45 pm. At 1.30 pm I go to a café for lunch. I work in a bank.

Put the sentences in this text in order.

My name is Montse.
I work in a bank.

8 Grammar: question forms

Ask Montse questions for these answers.

1 *What's your name?*
  Montse.

2 My name is Monse ?
  I work in a bank.

3 _____ ?
  I go to the bank at eight.

4 _____ ?
  I get to the bank at nine.

5 _____ ?
  I go to a cafe.

6 _____ ?
  At about six.

7 _____ ?
  I usually go to the cinema.

9 Listening

Listen to Seamus and complete the information below.

Breakfast	
Go to the office	
Get to the office	
Lunch	
Go home	
Spanish class	7.30
Back home	

10 Reading

Read the text below and look at the sentences. Write *True* or *False*.

1 Solopasta is open on Saturday. *True*
2 Upper Street Fish Shop is open on Monday morning. _____
3 Frederick's is closed on Sunday. _____
4 M'sieur Frogs is open from 7.00 pm to 11.30 pm on Tuesday. _____
5 Suruchi is open on Sunday evening. _____
6 Roxy Café-Cantina is closed from 3.30 pm to 5.30 pm on Friday. _____

Café Pasta 8 Theberton St, N1 (226 2211). Open 9.30am-11.30pm Mon-Sat; 9.30am-11pm Sun.
Frederick's Camden Passage, N1 (359 2888). Open 12noon-2.30pm, 7-11.15pm Mon-Sat; Closed Sun.
Moussaka On The Green 23 Islington Green, N1 (354 1952).
M'sieur Frogs 31a Essex Rd, N1 (226 3495). Open 7-11.30pm Mon-Sat; closed Sun.
Parveen Tandoori 6 Theberton St, N1 (226 0504). Open Sun-Thurs 6-11.45pm; 6pm-1am Fri, Sat.
Roxy Café-Cantina 297 Upper St, N1 (226 5746). Open 10.30am-3.30pm, 5.30-11.45pm Mon-Fri; 10.30am-11.45pm Sat; 10.30am-11pm Sun.
Solopasta 26 Liverpool Rd, N1 (359 7648). Open 5.30-10.30pm Mon-Sat; closed Sun.
Suruchi 18 Theberton St, N1 (359 8033). Open 12noon-2.30pm, 6-10.30pm every day.
Upper Street Fish Shop 324 Upper St, N1 (359 1401). Open 5.30-10pm Mon; 12noon-2pm (3pm Sat), 5.30-10pm Tues-Fri; closed Sun.

Unit 3

1 Numbers

Write the numbers in words.

Example: I am 17 (__seventeen__).

My name's André. I am 22 (_____) years old. I've got 2 (_____) brothers and sisters. My brother Jean-Luc is 20. (_____) My sister is 15 (_____). My father is 61 (_____) and my mother is 59 (_____). I'm a waiter. I work from 11 (_____) o'clock to 3.30 (_____) and from 8 (_____) o'clock to 12.30 (_____).

2 Vocabulary

Complete the pairs.

1 sister and   __brother__
2 father and   _____
3 son and   _____
4 grandmother and   _____
5 aunt and   _____
6 husband and   _____
7 girlfriend and   _____

3 Grammar: contractions

Write the full forms of the verbs.

1 She's a student.
   __She is a student.__

2 She's Japanese.
   _____

3 He's got two daughters.
   _____

4 She's married.
   _____

5 Her name's Eva.
   _____

6 His wife's name's Joan.
   _____

7 She's got Marie's book.
   _____

8 Ahmet's sister's twenty-one.
   _____

9 What's your father's name?
   _____

4 Reading

Read the text and write the questions.

> Adam Borntrager, of Medford, Wisconsin, USA, has 707 direct descendants. He has 11 children, 115 grandchildren, 529 great-grandchildren and 20 great-great-grandchildren.

1 __How many descendants has he got?__ 707
2 _____ 11
3 _____ 20
4 _____ 115

12

5 Grammar: possession

Look at the family tree and decide if the sentences are *True* or *False*. Correct the false sentences.

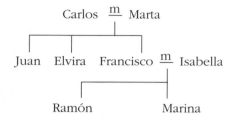

1 Carlos is Elvira's father.
   True

2 Marina is Isabella's mother.
   False. Marina is Isabella's daughter.

3 Juan is Elvira's brother.
   ___

4 Carlos is Ramón's father.
   ___

5 Isabella and Francisco are married.
   ___

6 Carlos and Marta have got three children.
   ___

7 Marta is Elvira's sister.
   ___

8 Francisco and Isabella have got one child.
   ___

9 Marta is Marina's grandmother.
   ___

10 Juan is Carlos's father.
   ___

11 Elvira is Juan's sister.
   ___

6 Listening

Listen to the cassette, and draw Jan's family tree.

7 Grammar: word order; possessive 's

Put the words in the correct order to make sentences.

1 has got two she brothers
   She has got two brothers.

2 Gary's Jan daughter is
   ___

3 are and Nat married Catherine
   ___

4 parents Nat's Gary are Doreen and
   ___

5 got he brother one has
   ___

6 Catherine children and haven't got Nat any
   ___

7 brother Jeff's is Nat
   ___

8 brothers two got Jan has
   ___

9 four got children have and Gary Doreen
   ___

8 Grammar: *have got*

1 Make five questions using this model.

How many	children sisters brothers babies	have has	I you she he we they	got?

Example:
1 *How many sisters have you got?*
2 ___ ?
3 ___ ?
4 ___ ?
5 ___ ?

2 Look again at this family tree from Exercise 5. Ask Elvira questions for these answers.

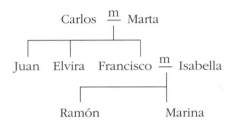

1 *Have you got any brothers?*
   Yes, I've got two brothers.
2 _____
   Carlos is my father.
3 _____ ?
   No, I haven't got any sisters.
4 _____ ?
   Marta is my mother.
5 _____ ?
   Yes, Francisco is married.
6 _____ ?
   Isabella is Francisco's wife.
7 _____ ?
   Yes, they've got two children.

9 Grammar: possession

Look at this picture and write the waiter's questions. Then write the answers.

1 (cereal)   *Whose is the cereal? Carl's.*
2 (orange juice) _____
3 (croissant)   _____
4 (egg)   _____
5 (toast)   _____
6 (coffee)   _____

10 Pronunciation: intonation

Listen to the cassette and repeat the questions.

Unit 4

1 Grammar: *this/these*; plurals

Change the sentences to the plural.

1 This magazine is German.
   These magazines are German.

2 Whose book is this?
   _____

3 It's Alfonso's.
   _____

4 This is a Spanish wine.
   _____

5 Is this your pen?
   _____

6 He's Portuguese.
   _____

7 Is your sister married?
   _____

8 Has this child got an English book?
   _____

9 This person is my friend.
   _____

2 Vocabulary: sports

Match the activity with the picture.

playing tennis   skiing
swimming   playing basketball
sailing   running
playing golf   horse-riding
playing baseball climbing
exercising

3 Grammar: adjectives and *-ing* forms

Complete the sentences.

1 I come from Italy but I don't like watching *Italian* films.
2 I come from Brazil but I don't like listening to _____ music.
3 I come from Greece but I don't like _____ _____ food.
4 She comes from _____ but she doesn't like _____ Australian beer.
5 He comes from _____ but he doesn't _____ _____ Spanish television.
6 I come from Egypt but I _____ like _____ _____ magazines.
7 We come _____ Portugal but we don't like _____ _____ wine.
8 He comes _____ _____ but he _____ _____ Dutch cheese.
9 She comes _____ _____ _____ _____ _____ _____ _____ Swiss chocolates.

4 Speaking

Listen to the cassette and respond.

Example:
CASSETTE: I like cooking. What about you?
YOU: I like cooking too.

1 _____ 2 _____ 3 *exercising* 4 _____ 5 _____ 6 _____

7 _____ 8 _____ 9 _____ 10 _____ 11 _____

5 Writing

Punctuate the text.

her name is carolien she comes from holland shes 20 years old shes got two brothers and a sister her sisters name is hilda caroliens a student she likes sports television and reading

6 Grammar: Present Simple

1 This is Carolien's daily routine. Write sentences about Carolien.

1 (7.00) *She gets up at seven o'clock.*
2 (7.30) _____
3 (8.30) _____
4 (9.00) _____
5 (1.00) _____
6 (2.00) _____
7 (3.00) _____
8 _____ *She does the housework.*
9 _____
10 _____
11 (12.00) _____

2 Look at Exercise 6:1 again. Now ask Carolien questions for these answers.

1 *What time do you get up?*
  At about 7.00.
2 _____?
  At about 7.30.
3 _____?
  At about 8.30.
4 _____?
  At about 9.00.

3 Now ask Hilda questions about Carolien.

1 *What time does Carolien have lunch?*
  At about 1.00.
2 _____?
  At about 2.00.
3 _____?
  At about 3.00.
4 _____?
  At about 12.00.

7 Listening

🎧 Listen to Hilda. What are the differences between Carolien's and Hilda's routines?

1 (get up) <u>Carolien gets up at 7.00 but Hilda gets up at 8.00.</u>
2 (breakfast) _____
3 (lunch) _____
4 (get home) _____
5 (housework) _____
6 (read) _____
7 (bed) _____

8 Reading

Read this text and put the pictures in order.

Tony Jackson is a triathlon athlete. Every Saturday he gets up at six and runs twenty miles before breakfast. After breakfast he swims 1,500 metres. Then he exercises in the gym for an hour. After lunch he sleeps for half an hour and then he gets on his bicycle and cycles 50 to 100 miles. Finally he finishes the day by walking five miles before bed.

9 Listening

🎧 Listen to the cassette and complete the chart. Put a tick (✓) for the things the four people like and a cross (✗) for the things they don't like.

	tea	coffee	beer	wine
Gül	✓	✓	✗	✗
Rosa				
André				
Leila				

10 Grammar: *to like*; *but*

Look at your answers for Exercise 9. Write sentences about Gül, Rosa, André, and Leila.

1 <u>Gül likes coffee but she doesn't like wine.</u>
2 Rosa _____
3 André _____
4 Leila _____

11 Pronunciation: word stress

Look at these countries and nationalities. Do they have the same stress or different stress?

1 America — American — *same*
2 Japan — Japanese — *different*
3 Italy — Italian
4 Brazil — Brazilian
5 Turkey — Turkish
6 Canada — Canadian
7 Egypt — Egyptian
8 Portugal — Portuguese
9 Kenya — Kenyan

Unit 5

1 Conversation

Complete the conversations, using *sorry*, *please*, *thank you*, and *excuse me*.

1 A: Coffee?
  B: No, _thank you._ .

2 A: _____.
  B: Yes?
  A: Have you got the time?
  B: No, _____.

3 A: Can I have the marmalade, _____?
  B: _____, I don't understand.
  A: The marmalade.
  B: Oh, here you are.
  A: _____.

4 A: _____, where is the post office?
  B: _____, I don't know.

5 A: It's nine fifteen!
  B: _____ I'm late.

2 Pronunciation: intonation

Listen to the cassette and repeat the words.

3 Numbers

Listen to the cassette and write the numbers.

1 A: How old is Karl?
  B: I think he's _13_ .

2 A: How many students are there?
  B: ____.

3 A: Good morning.
  B: Can I have ____ stamps, please?

4 A: How old are you?
  B: I'm ____. And you?
  A: I'm ____.

5 A: How much is that, please?
  B: £____ .

6 A: What time do you get home?
  B: Normally at ____.

7 A: What's your phone number?
  B: Have you got a pen?
  A: Yes.
  B: It's ____.

8 A: Excuse me, have you got the correct time?
  B: Yes, it's ____.
  A: Thank you.

9 A: Can I have ____ teas, ____ black coffees, and ____ white coffees, please.
  B: ____ teas?
  A: No, ____.

4 Conversation

1 Match the questions to the answers.

1 Is the shop open?   W-A-L-E-S.
2 Where do you come from?   Yes, two boys.
3 Anything else?   I'm 27.
4 How do you spell that?   Here you are.
5 What's your name?   Megan.
6 How old are you?   Yes, I am.
7 Can I have a bottle of milk? Wales.
8 Are you married?   Yes, it is.
9 Have you got any children?   No, thank you.

2 Now write two conversations from the questions and answers.

Conversation One
Is the shop open?   _Yes, it is._
_____   _____
_____   _____

Conversation Two
What's your name?   _Megan._
_____   _____
_____   _____
_____   _____
_____   _____
_____   _____

5 Reading

Read the text and answer the questions below.

> In Japanese *dozo* (please) and *arigato gozaimasu* (thank you) are very important words. The Japanese use them a lot. If you need to attract the attention of a shop assistant, it is polite to say *sumimasen* (excuse me). There is no word like 'Hello' in Japanese. The Japanese have a number of different expressions, depending on the time of day. For example, in the morning, they say *ohayo gozaimasu* and in the afternoon they say *konnichiwa*.

1 How do you say 'please' in Japanese?
   dozo.

2 What does *arigato gozaimasu* mean?
   _____

3 How do you say 'Excuse me' in Japanese?
   _____

4 How do the Japanese say 'Good morning'?
   _____

5 What does *konnichiwa* mean?
   _____

6 Dictionary work

1 Match the expressions to the definitions.
Note: *infml* = informal

1 bye   a shout used to call attention or to express surprise, interest, etc.
2 hi!   *infml* yes
3 ta   *infml* hello
4 hey!   *infml* thank you
5 yeah   *infml* goodbye

2 Now, re-write this conversation to make it more polite.

A: Hey!   *Excuse me.*
B: Yeah? _____
A: Have you got the time?
B: It's 5.45.
A: Ta.   _____
B: Bye.   _____
A: Bye.   _____

7 Pronunciation: vowel sounds

1 Put the words into the correct column according to the pronunciation.

tea know I hey! they we two hi! three do bye me to no say she buy

1 day	2 be	3 my	4 go	5 you
	tea			

2 🔊 Listen to the cassette and check your answers. Then listen again and repeat the words.

8 Writing

Put the information in the correct place in the form.

Canada   2 daughters   081 318 0122   34
Debbie Cartwright   married
234 West Green Rd, London N4 0ET

9 Grammar: verb review

Complete the text.

Debbie Cartwright c*omes* from Canada but she l_____ in London. She s_____ French and English. She _____ thirty-four and she _____ married. Her husband, Graham, _____ Australian and _____ a school teacher. They _____ _____ two daughters. Debbie and Graham both l_____ reading, travelling and l_____ to music.

19

1 Grammar: Past Simple

1 Match the verbs to the pictures.

walk   watch   cook   dance   listen   work   wash

1 watch
2 _____
3 _____
4 _____
5 _____
6 _____
7 _____

2 Now, write the verbs in the Past Simple.

watch   watched
_____   _____
_____   _____
_____   _____
_____   _____
_____   _____

3 Now listen to the cassette, and number the verbs in Exercise 1:2 in the correct order (1, 2, 3, etc).

4 Complete the letter using these verbs in the Past Simple.

visit   go   watch   read   write   do   walk
buy   have   do

> Monday June 23rd
>
> Dear Eva,
> How are you? What a busy weekend! On Saturday David had the car, so I _____ to the shops and I _____ cheese, ham, and tomatoes for a pizza. Then I _____ some work and _____ lunch. After lunch I _____ my parents. It was my mother's birthday. We _____ a video. – it was a birthday present. In the evening I _____ a long letter to my aunt. She's not very well. Yesterday I _____ my French homework. I've got an exam on Wednesday. And then I _____ a book, (the TV is broken) and _____ to the cinema in the evening. What did you do?
>
> Love,
> Ana

5 Write questions about Ana (in Exercise 1:4) for these answers.

1 *Why did she walk to the shops?*
  Because David had the car.
2 _____?
  Because she wanted to make a pizza.
3 _____?
  Because it was her mother's birthday.
4 _____?
  Because it was a birthday present.
5 _____?
  Because her aunt is not very well.
6 _____?
  Because she's got an exam on Wednesday.
7 _____?
  Because the TV is broken.

2 Reading

Read the text and then complete the lifeline for Armand Hammer.

Armand Hammer was born in the USA in 1898 and died on 10th December 1990. When he was twenty-one he took over his father's small chemical business and in 1919 he made his first million dollars.

In 1921 he visited the Soviet Union and started an import-export business. He married his first wife, Olga, in 1923 and they lived in Moscow.

He went back to the US in 1931 with a collection of Russian art, and made another million dollars.

In 1956 he started another international business: petroleum.

He visited many countries, including China, Libya, and Afghanistan. In an average year he travelled a quarter of a million miles. And he personally knew many world leaders including Lenin, Presidents Kennedy and Nixon, and Colonel Gadaffi.

'People ask me: are you lucky?' he once said. 'I tell them that when I work fourteen hours a day, seven days a week, I get lucky.'

Include this information in the lifeline:

he started a petroleum business
he married Olga
he went back to the USA
he was born
he made his first million
he died
he visited the Soviet Union

Life of Armand Hammer

1990
1956
1931
1923
1921
1919
1898 He was born

3 Listening

🔊 **Listen to the cassette and complete the text. Then answer the puzzle.**

He _____ _____ _____ England _____ April _____. He _____ _____ _____ _____ London. _____ _____ _____ _____ _____ writer. _____ _____ _____ _____ Anne. _____ _____ _____ plays. _____ _____ _____ _____.

Puzzle: Who was he? _____

4 Grammar: Past Simple

Look at the lifeline of the Spanish writer Miguel de Cervantes. Complete the sentences about his life.

1616 — Died
1615 — Don Quixote (Part 2)
1605 — Don Quixote (Part 1)
1584 — Married (Catalina)
1569 — Moved (Italy)
1547 — Born (Spain)

(sixteen plays)

1 He **was born in Spain** in 1547.
2 He _____ 1569.
3 He _____ in 1584.
4 He _____ plays.
5 He wrote _____ in 1605.
6 _____ in 1615.
7 _____ in 1616.

Puzzle: What is the same in Shakespeare's life and in Cervantes' life?
They both _____

5 Writing

Punctuate this text.

christopher marlowe was an english poet and dramatist he was born in canterbury in 1564 his father was a shoemaker he went to cambridge university he wrote doctor faustus in 1590 in 1593 he was killed in a fight in deptford

Puzzle: What is the same in Marlowe's life and Shakespeare's life? _They were both_

6 Speaking

Listen to the cassette and respond.

Example: 1 4th January
CASSETTE: What's the date?
YOU: It's the fourth of January.

2 (12th May)
3 (21st August)
4 (16th December)
5 (2nd March)
6 (5th July)
7 (23rd April)
8 (30th November)

7 Grammar: prepositions of time

Complete the sentences with prepositions.

1 Armand Hammer was born _in_ 1898.
2 He died ____ December 10th 1990.
3 Shakespeare was born ____ April.
4 Galileo and Shakespeare were both born ____ 1564.
5 I read *Doctor Faustus* ____ Monday.
6 Shakespeare died ____ April 23rd.
7 Cervantes went to Italy ____ 1569.

8 Dictionary work

Match the definition with the job.

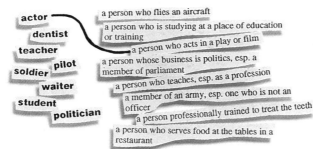

actor — a person who acts in a play or film
dentist
teacher
pilot — a person who flies an aircraft
soldier
waiter
student — a person who is studying at a place of education or training
politician — a person whose business is politics, esp. a member of parliament

a person who teaches, esp. as a profession
a member of an army, esp. one who is not an officer
a person professionally trained to treat the teeth
a person who serves food at the tables in a restaurant

9 Grammar: possessive adjectives; *this/these*

Complete the sentences.

1 This is Sumiko. And this is _her_ daughter.
2 This is Wolf. And this is ____ wife.
3 This is Ivan. And these are ____ children.
4 My name's Aneke. And these are ____ parents.
5 This is Brahim. And ____ is ____ mother.
6 This is Kazumi. And ____ ____ ____ sisters.

Unit 7

1 Vocabulary

Number these places and things on the ship.

1 bar 2 colour television
3 private bathroom
4 swimming pool 5 hairdresser
6 twin-beds
7 restaurant 8 duty-free shops
9 cinema
10 clinic 11 nursery

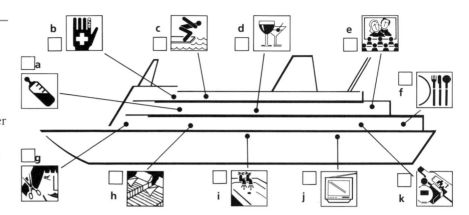

2 Reading and writing

Read this description of the ship and complete the postcard below.

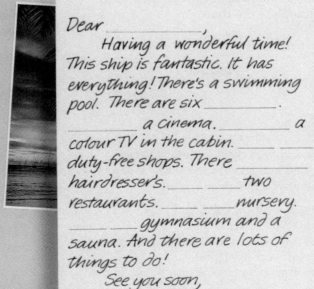

THE CRUISE OF A LIFETIME!

Enjoy style and comfort at prices you can afford! The SS OBERON invites you to savour the magic of tropical nights on the high seas. Join us for the cruise of a lifetime, and enjoy these five-star facilities:

★ two top class restaurants and six bars
★ air-conditioned cinema
★ swimming pool
★ double- and single-bedded cabins with or without private bathrooms
★ colour television in every cabin
★ sauna, jacuzzi and gym
★ clinic and children's nursery
★ a selection of shops where duty-free goods are available
★ hairdresser's

Consult your travel agent now! BO

Dear _____,
Having a wonderful time! This ship is fantastic. It has everything! There's a swimming pool. There are six _____. _____ a cinema. _____ a colour TV in the cabin. _____ duty-free shops. There _____ hairdresser's. _____ two restaurants. _____ nursery. _____ gymnasium and a sauna. And there are lots of things to do!
   See you soon,
      _____

3 Grammar: prepositions of place

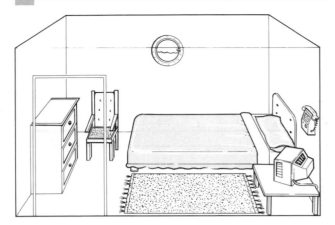

Look at the picture of the cabin, and decide if these sentences are *True* or *False*.

1 The television is under the window. __False__
2 The bed is next to the door. _____
3 The table is next to the bed. _____
4 The television is under the table. _____
5 The bed is in the cabin. _____
6 The telephone is on the table. _____
7 The window is above the bed. _____

4 Reading

Read the information about Greta, Brita and Wim and complete the chart.

	Greta	Brita	Wim
Month		August	
City			
Hotel			

Greta, Brita and Wim went to three different places for their holidays. They went in different months and stayed in different hotels.

- One person went on holiday in June.
- Wim didn't stay in the Grand.
- The person who went to Cairo went in August.
- One person went to Madrid.
- The person who went to Venice stayed in the Excelsior.
- Brita went on holiday in August.
- The person who stayed in the Ritz went in July.
- Greta didn't go to Venice.
- One person stayed in the Grand.

5 Listening

📼 Now listen to the cassette to see if your answers to Exercise 4 were correct.

6 Grammar: Past Simple negative

Write sentences about Greta, Brita, and Wim using *didn't*.

1 Wim/Cairo
   Wim didn't go to Cairo.
2 Brita/Excelsior
   _____
3 Greta/Madrid/June
   _____
4 Wim/Madrid
   _____
5 Brita/Cairo/July
   _____
6 Greta/Venice
   _____

7 Grammar: possessive adjectives

Complete the sentences with *my, your, his, her, our, their*.

1 I'd like some ice in __my__ orange juice.
2 We'd like breakfast in _____ room.
3 Would you like wine with _____ meal?
4 He'd like bacon with _____ eggs.
5 The children would like a TV in _____ room.
6 We'd like milk on _____ cereal.
7 Would you like tonic with _____ gin?
8 They'd like lunch in _____ cabin.
9 She'd like lemon in _____ tea.

8 Listening

🔲 Listen to the cassette. Underline the words you hear.

1 <u>*would you like*</u> or *do you like?*
2 *they're* or *their?*
3 *he's* or *his?*
4 *we'd like* or *we like?*
5 *this* or *these?*
6 *would you like* or *do you like?*
7 *he's* or *his?*
8 *I'd like* or *I like?*
9 *is* or *was?*
10 *there's* or *these?*
11 *is* or *was?*

9 Reading

Hotels in Beijing

Capital Airport Guest Hotel
Next to Capital Airport
Tel. 555177
The Airport Guest House is conveniently situated less than a kilometre from the international terminal and offers postal facilities.

Lüsongyuan Guest House
22 Jiao Dao Kou, Ban Chang Alley
This tiny guest house is centrally located.

Jianguo Hotel
8 Jianguomenwai Street
Tel. 5002233
Located in central Beijing, this hotel has Chinese, Japanese and Western restaurants.

The Great Wall Hotel, Beijing
A6 Donghuan Beilu.
Tel. 5005566
The Great Wall Hotel offers its guests a full range of amenities including a health club, shops and conference facilities. The hotel can also arrange sightseeing tours.

Friendship Hotel
3 Hai Dian Road Tel. 890621
The Friendship Hotel has tennis courts and postal and conference facilities. It is located in western Beijing.

From *Beijing* (Tourist Publications)

Read the information and find the correct hotels.

1 A hotel that is next to the airport.
   Capital Airport Guest House.

2 a hotel that has a Japanese restaurant.
   _____

3 a hotel that has tennis courts.
   _____

4 a hotel that is small and central.
   _____

5 a hotel with a health club.
   _____

10 Conversation

Read the information about The Great Wall Hotel (in Exercise 9) and complete this telephone conversation.

RECEPTIONIST: Hello. The Great Wall Hotel.
YOU: *Where is the Great Wall Hotel?*
RECEPTIONIST: A6 Donhuan Beilu.
YOU: _____?
RECEPTIONIST: Yes, there is air-conditioning in every room.
YOU: _____?
RECEPTIONIST: No, there isn't a swimming pool.
YOU: _____?
RECEPTIONIST: Yes, there is television in every room.
YOU: _____?
RECEPTIONIST: Yes, there is a health club.
YOU: _____?
RECEPTIONIST: Yes, there are rooms with private bathrooms.
YOU: _____?
RECEPTIONIST: A double room with a private bathroom is $120.
YOU: Thank you for your help.
RECEPTIONIST: You're welcome. Goodbye.

11 Speaking

🔲 Listen to the cassette and answer the questions.

Example:
CASSETTE: Would you like a double bed or a single bed?
YOU: I'd like a double bed, please.

Unit 8

1 Vocabulary: clothes

Look at the pictures and complete the words about clothes.

1 s **k i r t**
2 s _ _ _ _
3 s _ _ _ _ _ _
4 s _ _ _ s
5 _ _ ss
6 _ _ _ _ s _ _ s
7 s _ _ _ _ s
8 _ _ _ _ _ s
9 _ _ _ _ _ _ s

2 Reading

1 Match the picture to the description.

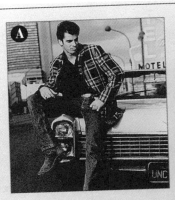

1 Bob wears bottle-green denim jacket £69 by Paul Smith from Paul Smith, London and Nottingham; white cotton T-shirt from £6.99 and black denim jeans from £39.99, both by Levi's from all good casual clothing shops. Emma wears ink-dyed denim jacket £107 and matching miniskirt £52, both by Katherine Hamnett, London and Glasgow.

2 Bob wears blue/orange tartan single-breasted cotton jacket £417 by Katherine Hamnett and Browns, London, and Katherine Hamnett, Glasgow; black cotton shirt £55 by Christopher New from Christopher New, London; black jeans from £39.99 by Levi's from all good casual clothing shops; brown suede cowboy boots and black leather belt from Kensington Market, London.

3 Emma wears gold stretch evening dress £153 by Katherine Hamnett from Katherine Hamnett and Browns, London, and Katherine Hamnett, Glasgow. Will wears a black single-breasted suit and white cotton shirt £65, both by Jasper Conran from Jasper Conran and Harrods, London, and Cruise, Glasgow.

From Arena

2 Now answer these questions.

1 How much is Bob's T-shirt? _____
2 What colour is Will's shirt? _____
3 Where can you buy Bob's jeans? _____

3 Pronunciation /ɑ:/

🔊 **Listen and circle the words with /ɑ:/.**

1 (Mark's) (party) is on Saturday.
2 Her father's car is black.
3 Charles started work in March.
4 My aunt can't dance.
5 Martha and Mary aren't from France.
6 There's a bar in the car park.
7 Can I have your landing card?

4 Grammar: negative forms

Write these sentences in the negative.

1 He's a student.
   He isn't a student.

2 I've got a car.

3 She can speak German.

4 They are brothers.

5 Eric's got a video.

6 We like playing football.

7 They live in London.

8 Virginia works in a bank.

9 I smoke.

5 Listening

🔊 **Listen to the conversation on the cassette. What are they going to give Sheila?**

1 chocolates
2 a compact disc
3 perfume
4 flowers
5 a book
6 a cassette
7 a Chinese meal

6 Grammar: *going to* (future)

Elena Costakis is a dancer. Look at the information below and make sentences about Elena's plans for next week.

1 (fly) *She's going to fly to Rome on Sunday.*
2 (see) _____
3 (dance) _____
4 (have dinner) _____
5 (stay) _____
6 (buy) _____
7 (meet) _____

7 Conversation

Complete the interview with Elena about her plans. It is Saturday 15 June.

INTERVIEWER: Well, Elena. You are going to dance in Rome next week, is that right?
ELENA: _Yes, I am._
INTERVIEWER: Are you going to fly?
ELENA: _____.
INTERVIEWER: What are you going to do in Rome?
ELENA: _____.
INTERVIEWER: Where_____ dance?
ELENA: _____.
INTERVIEWER: And after Rome?
ELENA: _____ fly _____.
INTERVIEWER: What _____?
ELENA: I'm going to meet _____.
INTERVIEWER: Why_____ your bank manager?
ELENA: I'm going to buy a villa on Mykonos.
INTERVIEWER: Well, good luck, Elena. And thanks very much.

8 Writing

1 Read Alfredo's invitation to Elena in Exercise 6. Then read the invitation from Elena's bank manager and answer the question.

> Athens
> June 3rd
>
> Dear Ms Costakis,
>
> I'm pleased to hear that you will be in Athens this month. Would you like to have lunch with me on Friday June 21st? If you like, I can meet you at your hotel at 1.00pm.
>
>   With best wishes,
>   Constantin Benaki

Which is more formal? Alfredo's letter or Constantin's letter?

○ 2 Re-write Alfredo's note to make it more formal.
○ 3 Re-write Constantin's note to make it more informal.

9 Speaking

🔊 Listen and make invitations.

Example:
CASSETTE: have lunch
YOU: Would you like to have lunch with me?

10 Grammar: short answers

Write short answers to these questions.

1 Is this Exercise 10? _Yes, it is._
2 Is this Unit 10? _____?
3 Are you a student of English? _____
4 Can you read this? _____
5 Has this book got pictures? _____
6 Did you do Unit 3? _____
7 Are you going to do Unit 9? _____
8 Does this book cost £100? _____
9 Is this the last exercise in this unit? _____

11 Puzzle

Can you solve this puzzle?

I can fly but I can't walk.
I can hear but I can't talk.
I can hunt but I can't see.
I can hang by my feet from a tree.
What am I?

1 Grammar: Past Simple

Put the sentences into the past.

1 They play tennis.
   They played tennis.

2 I drive a car.
   _____

3 Does she speak Hindi?
   _____

4 He reads Arabic.
   _____

5 I put the film in the camera.
   _____

6 Do you like the play?
   _____

7 They don't go to school.
   _____

8 Does he smoke?
   _____

9 Anna writes music and Ben plays it.
   _____

2 Speaking

■ **Listen and reply to the assistant.**

ASSISTANT: Good morning. Can I help you?
YOU: I'd like to buy a film for this camera.
ASSISTANT: Prints or slides?
YOU: _____
ASSISTANT: Black and white or colour?
YOU: _____
ASSISTANT: How many? 12, 24, or 36?
YOU: _____
ASSISTANT: That will be £4.75, please.
YOU: _____

3 Vocabulary

Complete the instructions using these verbs and nouns.

Verbs		Nouns	
move	open	face	toes
wash	clean	foot	teeth
touch		mouth	

_____ your _____

_____ your _____

_____ your _____

_____ your _____

_____ your _____

29

4 Reading

1 Match these instructions with the correct picture.

Stand up straight with your feet apart.
Bend your knees slightly.
Bend down and touch the floor with your palms.
Push the floor gently, and stretch the back and legs.

2 Now put the words in these instructions in the correct order.

1 back your lie on
   Lie on your back.

2 your knee left lift
   _____

3 your down pull knee
   _____

4 right stretch your leg
   _____

5 lift now right knee your
   _____

6 down and pull knee your your leg left stretch
   _____

3 Match the instructions in Exercise 4:2 with the correct picture in Exercise 4:1.

5 Grammar: prepositions of place

Look at the pictures and write sentences.

1.
2.
3.
4.
5.
6.

1 S is *between R and T.*
2 X _____
3 Z _____
4 D _____
5 J _____
6 V *is on the right of U.*
7 V _____
8 M _____
9 F _____

6 Listening

📼 **Look at the picture and listen to the cassette. Match the names to the people.**

Annie   Annie's father   Uncle Jack   Aunt Vera
Sylvia   Eddie

30

7 Pronunciation: vowel sounds

Circle the word which doesn't rhyme.

Example: grey   day   (buy)
          /greɪ/ /deɪ/ /baɪ/

1 toe   shoe   go
2 foot   put   shut
3 ear   hair   beer
4 right straight eight
5 suit   feet   eat
6 tie   buy   knee
7 move   above   love
8 to live five give

8 Grammar: can/can't

Make questions and answers using *can* and *can't*.

1 speak French?   German
   Can you speak French?
   No, I can't, but I can speak German.

2 speak Portuguese?   understand Portuguese
   _____
   _____

3 squash?   tennis
   _____
   _____

4 a bus?   a car
   _____
   _____

5 dance?   sing
   _____
   _____

6 the guitar?   the piano
   _____
   _____

7 a computer?   a calculator
   _____
   _____

9 Listening

 Listen to the cassette and decide if you hear *can* or *can't*.

1 *can't*
2 _____
3 _____
4 _____
5 _____
6 _____
7 _____
8 _____
9 _____

10 Writing

Change these instructions into informal English, using *don't*.

1 NO SMOKING
2 SILENCE

Don't smoke.

3 No Photography
4 PLEASE do not touch the exhibits
5 KEEP OFF THE GRASS
6 EATING AND DRINKING PROHIBITED
7 NO PARKING
8 No ball games
9 SINGING AND DANCING STRICTLY PROHIBITED

Unit 10

1 Vocabulary

Match each word in list A to its example in list B.

A	B
1 spelling	a student
2 pronunciation	b books
3 script	c book
4 syllable	d n
5 vowel	e W–O–R–D
6 consonant	f *Word*
7 stress	g did
8 auxiliary	h /wɜːd/
9 singular	i 'student
10 plural	j e

(1 spelling — f *Word*)

2 Pronunciation: syllables

1 Count the syllables in these words.

1 nationality __5__
2 language ____
3 syllable ____
4 vowel ____
5 people ____
6 name ____
7 television ____
8 telephone ____
9 year ____

2 ▢ Listen to the cassette and mark the stress on these words.

1 birthday
2 fifteenth
3 July
4 hamburger
5 ice-cream
6 perfume
7 magazine
8 Chinese
9 receptionist

3 Vocabulary: plurals

Write the plural of these words.

1 girl __girls__
2 boy ____
3 baby ____
4 family ____
5 man ____
6 woman ____
7 child ____
8 person ____
9 foot ____

4 Reading

Read the text below and then choose the correct answers to the questions.

1 How many people speak Hungarian?
 a 12,000,000
 b 500,000
 c 12,500,000
2 Hungarians write in a:
 a Slavonic script
 b Roman script
 c Hungarian script
3 Why is Hungarian difficult for English speakers?
 a the pronunciation
 b the grammar only
 c the spelling
 d the vocabulary and the grammar
4 How many letters are there in the Hungarian alphabet?
 a 8
 b 15
 c 40

THE HUNGARIAN LANGUAGE

Hungarian (or Magyar) is the language of about 12,000,000 people, and is spoken mainly in Hungary, as well as in parts of Czechoslovakia, Romania, and Yugoslavia. There are also about half a million Hungarian speakers in the United States.

Hungarian is in the same family of languages as Finnish. This makes it a difficult language for English speakers to learn because the vocabulary is very different from other European languages. There is no verb *to have* in Hungarian. To express 'possession' Hungarians use the verb *to be*.

To English speakers the grammar of Hungarian is very difficult too. There are no auxiliaries. Instead, each verb has many different endings. Hungarian has about twenty-five noun cases.

In the eleventh century the Hungarians adopted a Roman script consisting of forty letters, including fifteen vowels and eight double consonants. The spelling is phonetic. Stress is always on the first vowel of a word.

5 Writing

○ **Write about your language. (If you are Hungarian, write about English!) Before you start, think about these questions.**

How many people speak your language?
Is it easy or difficult to learn?
How do you write it?
How many vowels and consonants has it got?

6 Listening

1 📼 **Listen to the cassette and answer these questions.**

1 How many people are there?
2 What are their names?

2 📼 **Listen again, and answer these questions:**

1 Who works with Martin?
2 Who doesn't like rock 'n roll?
3 Who would like orange juice?
4 Who's from Australia?
5 Who's Martin's girlfriend?

7 Speaking

📼 **Look at these expressions from the conversation in Exercise 6.**

Oh really?
I think so.

Now listen to the cassette and respond, using *I think so* or *Oh really*?

Example:
CASSETTE: Have you got any orange juice?
YOU: I think so.
CASSETTE: Martin works with Bob.
YOU: Oh really?

8 Grammar: review

Put one of the words in each space to complete the text.

met from was in graduated wrote music on died studying started teacher

Zoltán Kodály, composer and musicologist, *was* born in Hungary ____ December 16th, 1882. He studied _____ in Budapest. He _____ collecting Hungarian folk songs in 1905. In 1906 he _____ from Budapest University. In the same year he _____ Béla Bartók. After _____ in Paris for a short time, he became a _____ of music at the Budapest Academy of Music. He worked there _____ 1907 to 1941. In 1926 he _____ a comic opera, Háry János. His symphony was first performed __ 1961. He _____ in Budapest in March, 1967.

9 Puzzle

Can you answer this question.

Who is my sister's mother's husband's wife's daughter's brother?

Unit 11

1 Vocabulary: describing people

1 Complete the lists with the correct nouns and adjectives.

Noun	Adjective
education	*educated*
religion	_____
_____	intelligent
_____	affectionate
politics	_____
_____	sincere
_____	attractive
_____	stupid
humour	_____
love	_____
_____	beautiful
_____	professional

2 Circle the correct word in the sentences.

1 He is very stupidity/(stupid).
2 I am interested in political/politics.
3 What is your religion/religious?
4 Einstein was very intelligence/intelligent.
5 Have you got a sense of humour/humorous?

2 Grammar: *to be; have got*

Complete the text with *is*, *are*, or *has got*.

Bettina *is* 22 years old. She ____ a medical student. She ____ very attractive. She ____ red hair. Her eyes ____ green. She ____ tall. She ____ a nice personality: she ____ sincere and intelligent.
Eric ____ very good-looking, and he ____ a good sense of humour. He ____ about 1.60 m tall. His hair ____ dark and he ____ brown eyes. He ____ twenty-nine and he ____ married. He ____ a job in a bank.

3 Listening

🔊 Listen to the cassette and underline the words you hear in the three descriptions.

1 tall short good-looking beautiful handsome blue eyes brown eyes dark hair fair hair
2 sincere educated kind intelligent affectionate attractive slim not very slim
3 attractive not very attractive affectionate not very affectionate beautiful not very beautiful intelligent not very intelligent

4 Writing

Put these sentences in the correct order. Make three paragraphs.

The second time we met was five years later.
This time she was interested, but I was married.
My marriage was finished and I was lonely.
I liked her immediately.
It was my twenty-sixth birthday party.
Five years later we met again.
She was eighteen and I was twenty-one.
But she was a happily married twenty-eight-year-old, with two children.
The first time I met Celia we were both students.
I wonder when we'll meet again?
But she wasn't interested.

Paragraph 1
The first time I met Celia we were both students.
_____
_____

Paragraph 2
_____
_____
_____

Paragraph 3
_____
_____
I wonder when we'll meet again?

5 Grammar: subject and object pronouns

TV TONIGHT

8.30 - Sibly Hall

The story: Alan loves Patty, his beautiful sister-in-law. Patty is married to George. George likes Eleanor – she works with George – but Eleanor lives with her boyfriend Gary. Gary works with Rita and Joe. Rita and Joe play tennis with George and Patty. Gary is on holiday. Meanwhile, Eleanor meets tall, handsome Nigel. She doesn't know that Nigel works with Gary.

Tonight: Eleanor visits Nigel at his office …

9.30 - News and Weather

1 Read the text and explain the relationships between the people. Make sentences using *he/him, she/her, they/them*.

1 Alan/Patty.
   He loves her.

2 Patty/George
   _____

3 George/Eleanor
   _____

4 Eleanor/Gary
   _____

5 Gary/Rita and Joe
   _____

6 Rita and Joe/George and Patty
   _____

7 Eleanor/Nigel
   _____

8 Nigel/Gary
   _____

6 Grammar: Past Simple + *ago*

Write the dates and make questions and answers.

1 Patty married George in 1985.
   When did Patty marry George?
   She married him __ years ago.

2 Eleanor met Gary in 1988.
   _____?
   _____.

3 Rita and her husband parted in 1989.
   _____?
   _____.

4 Joe met Rita last December.
   _____?
   _____.

5 Gary went on holiday last _____.
   _____?
   _____ one month ago.

6 Gary came home on _____.
   _____?
   _____ two days ago.

7 Pronunciation: sentence stress

🔊 **Listen to the cassette. Decide if the verb is *stressed* or *unstressed*.**

1 (is)   Patty is married to George. **unstressed**
2 (is)   Is Patty married? _____
3 (is)   Yes, she is. _____
4 (are)   Alan and Patty are single. _____
5 (aren't) No, they aren't. _____
6 (are)   Yes, they are. _____
7 (is)   Gary is on holiday. _____
8 (has)   Has Rita got a daughter? _____
9 (has)   Yes she has. _____

8 Reading

Read the poem and choose the correct answer to the question.

Long Ago

I'd like to speak of this memory,

but it's so faded now – as though nothing's left –

because it was long ago, in my adolescent years.

A skin as though of jasmine ...

that August evening – was it August? –

I can still just recall the eyes: blue, I think they were ...

Ah yes, blue: a sapphire blue.

C.P.Cavafy (1863–1933)

How long ago was 'that August evening'?

a in the 1860s?
b in the 1880s?
c in the 1930s?

9 Grammar: *was/were*

Complete the sentences with *was* or *were*.

1 What _was_ the last film you saw?
2 I liked her because she _____ very sincere.
3 Where _____ you born?
4 Both Cavafy and Seferis _____ Greek.
5 Cleopatra _____ not very beautiful.
6 We met when we _____ at school.
7 I _____ born in 1965.
8 How long ago _____ you in Alexandria?
9 I think his eyes _____ blue.

10 Speaking

Listen to the cassette and respond. Choose the correct answer from the list.

American Spanish Egyptian singers short
a writer married Austrian

Example:
CASSETTE: Was Cleopatra Italian?
YOU: No, she wasn't. She was Egyptian.

11 Reading

Have you got a sense of humour? Match the texts to the pictures.

"Go quickly, my husband is coming."
"Separate futures, please."
"Business is terrible."

a

b

c

Unit 12

1 Vocabulary: transport

Write the correct words next to the pictures to complete the text.

I used seven different forms of transport on my holiday in Egypt. First I took a **plane** to Cairo. In Cairo I used the _____ to visit different places in the city. From Cairo I went to the Pyramids by _____. Then I took a _____ to Aswan. From Aswan I went to Luxor by _____. In Luxor I rented a _____ and went to the Valley of the Kings. Finally, I returned to Cairo by _____.

2 Grammar: countable and uncountable nouns

Read the recipe for Imam Bayıldı. Then complete the two lists with the things from the recipe.

Uncountable
olive oil

Countable
aubergines

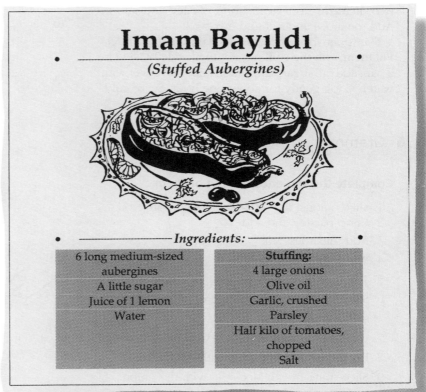

Imam Bayıldı
(Stuffed Aubergines)

Ingredients:

6 long medium-sized aubergines	**Stuffing:**
A little sugar	4 large onions
Juice of 1 lemon	Olive oil
Water	Garlic, crushed
	Parsley
	Half kilo of tomatoes, chopped
	Salt

3 Listening

Listen to the conversation. Make a list of the things they *have got* and the things they *haven't got*.

	YES	NO
	sugar	

4 Grammar: *some/any*

Now look at the list in Exercise 3 and make sentences.

1 (sugar) *They've got some sugar.*
2 (aubergines) *They haven't got any aubergines.*
3 (olive oil) _____
4 (salt) _____
5 (onions) _____
6 (tomatoes) _____
7 (lemons) _____
8 (garlic) _____
9 (parsley) _____

5 Reading

Now read the instructions for Imam Bayıldı. Then, using a dictionary, match the verbs from the recipe with the pictures (right).

To make the stuffing: Slice the onions. Fry them gently in olive oil. Add garlic and stir for a minute or two. Remove from heat. Chop parsley and add it. Add tomatoes and salt and mix well.

Slice open the aubergines and take out the centres. Fill them with the stuffing. Put them side by side in a pan, add oil, sugar, salt, lemon juice and cover with water. Cook gently for about one hour. Serve cold.

1 slice
2 fry
3 add
4 remove
5 chop
6 stir
7 mix
8 fill
9 cook
10 serve

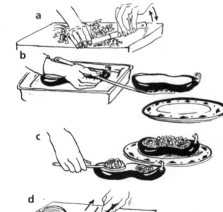

6 Grammar: *it/them*

Complete the sentences with *it* or *them*.

1 Slice onions. Fry *them* gently in olive oil.
2 Chop parsley and add *it* .
3 Add tomatoes. Stir ____ well.
4 Wash six aubergines. Slice ____ open.
5 Take some parsley. Chop ____ well.
6 Slice open one aubergine. Fill ____ with the stuffing.
7 Chop one onion. Mix ____ with the tomatoes.
8 Fry the eggs. Serve ____ with the bacon.
9 Slice some bread. Mix ____ with the onion.
10 Chop some garlic. Add ____ to the stuffing.

7 Pronunciation: sentence stress

🔊 **Listen to the cassette. Decide if the words are *stressed* or *unstressed*.**

1 (some) We need some sugar. *unstressed*
2 (any) Have we got any cheese? _____
3 (any) No, we haven't got any. _____
4 (have) Yes, we have. _____
5 (some) We need some onions _____
6 (do) Do we need any parsley? _____
7 (do) Yes, we do. _____

8 Speaking

🔊 **Listen to the cassette and respond, using adjectives from the list.**

tasteless   slow   unfriendly   dirty   expensive
clean   cold   cheap

Example: CASSETTE: Was the hotel clean?
         YOU: No, it was dirty.

9 Grammar: prepositions of place

Complete the sentences with *next to / near / not far from / a long way from*.

1 Catalonia is a region of Spain _____ Aragon.
2 Spain is _____ New Zealand.
3 Tarragona is _____ Barcelona.
4 Altafulla is _____ Tarragona.

10 Reading

1 Read the text and decide which is the best title for it.

Titles:
a Catalonia
b Catalan Cooking
c *Parrillada*.

> Catalonia is a region of 12,000 square miles between the Pyrenees in the north and the Costa Dorada in the south. Catalan cuisine has a long history: the first cookbook published in Spain was written in the Catalan language in the early fourteenth century.
>
> There are six important ingredients in Catalan cooking: olive oil, garlic, onions, tomatoes, nuts, and dried fruits, particularly raisins and prunes. In addition, the four traditional herbs are oregano, rosemary, thyme and bay leaves.
>
> Typical foods are fish, rabbit and pork. Red peppers stuffed with cod is a typical dish. Catalans love grilled dishes too: *parrillada*, a combination of grilled shellfish, or lamb, is a great favourite.

2 Put the food vocabulary from the text into the correct column.

vegetables	meat	fish	herbs	dried fruit	others
onions					

11 Writing

○ **Now, write about the typical food of your country or region. (If you are Catalan, write about English food!) Before you start think about these questions.**

What are the important ingredients?
What are some typical dishes?
What is your favourite dish?
How do you make it?

Unit 13

1 Vocabulary: weather

1 Write the nouns for the weather symbols.

1 ☔ _rain_   3 ☁ _____   5 ❄ _____

2 ☀ _____   4 ➡ _____   6 ▨ _____

2 Use your dictionary. Match these words with the pictures.

shower   hail   mist   ice   thunderstorm   breeze

1 _shower_   3 _____   5 _____

2 _____   4 _____   6 _____

3 Make adjectives.

1 mist _misty_   5 shower _____
2 sun _____   6 storm _____
3 cloud _____ 7 ice _____
4 fog _____   8 wind _____

2 Listening

🔊 Look at the map of Canada and listen to the weather forecast. Mark the weather on the map using the symbols.

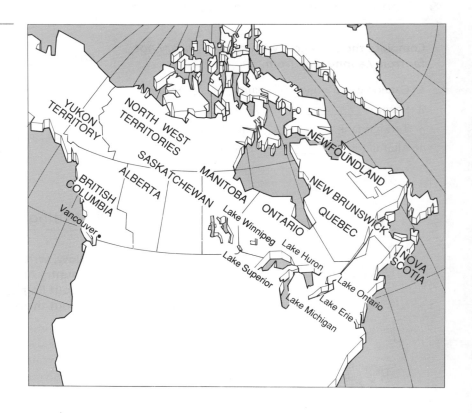

Key

Unit 0

1 Down
1 TELEVISION
Across
1 TAXI
2 CINEMA
3 TELEPHONE
4 CASSETTE
5 VIDEO
6 RADIO
7 BUS
8 POLICE
9 CHOCOLATE
10 SANDWICH

3 1 VIDEO
2 BANK
3 HOTEL
4 TENNIS
5 FOOTBALL
6 RESTAURANT
7 HOSPITAL
8 PIZZA
9 CIGARETTE

Unit 1

1 1 sugar
2 milk
3 cereal
4 coffee or tea
5 toast and marmalade
6 bread and butter
7 eggs and bacon

2 1 a small apple
2 six hot chocolates
3 an egg
4 an orange juice
5 two white coffees
6 a croissant
7 three black teas
8 an English breakfast
9 three big potatoes

3 1 cereal, milk, cream, toast, jam, marmalade, honey, tea, coffee, milk, sugar, eggs, bacon, sausages, orange juice, muesli, yoghurt, coffee, milk, sugar.
2 1 c 2 a 3 b

4 2 Good morning, madam
Good morning. Breakfast please.
Coffee or tea?
Tea, please.
3 Two eggs, please.
Anything else?
No, thank you. That's all.
4 Tea or coffee?
Coffee, please.
With milk?
Yes, please.
Sugar?
No, no sugar, thanks.

5 Room number: 301
Breakfast for 2
2 black coffees 1 toast and marmalade and 1 egg and bacon

7 3 2+7=9
4 3x2=6
5 9-8=1
6 9/3=3
7 9510362
8 855924

8 a 0223
b 315 697
c 017 569 215
d 39 01 56
e 318 01 22
f 018 543 909
g 010 39
h 010 349 456 209
i 010 648 98 971
j 999

9 2 What's your name?
3 Where do you come from?
4 How do you spell Italy?
5 What's your telephone number?
6 What's the code for Italy?

10 2 Norway
3 Italy
4 Australia
5 England
6 Canada
7 Japan
8 Brazil
9 Portugal

11 2 It's the Hilton Hotel.
3 I'm Mark Andrews.
4 He's a waiter.
5 You're a student.
6 Is this an English breakfast?
7 Do you have coffee with milk?
8 How many sugars do you have?

Unit 2

1
2
1 3 False
4 False
5 True
6 False
7 True
8 True
9 False
10 False
11 True
12 True

2
2 film, post office (for example: pubs, cafés – beer, coffee)

3 2 is
3 are
4 are
5 am
6 is
7 is
8 is
9 is, are

4 In Ireland shops are open from nine to six, and banks are open from 9.30 am to 12.30 Monday to Friday and they open again from 1.30 to 3.00. Shops are open on Saturdays but banks are closed on Saturdays and Sundays. Cinemas are open from 2.30 to 10.30, and pubs are open from 11.00 am to 12.00 pm every day except Sunday when they close at 11.00.

5 2. In Italy banks are open from 8.30 am to 1.30 pm.
3. In Milan offices are open from 8.00 am to 2.30 pm.
4 In Italy shops are closed from 1.00 pm to 4.30 pm.
5 In Rome post offices are open on Saturday from 8.00 am to 2.00 pm.
6 In Italy museums are closed on Monday.

7 My name is Montse. I work in a bank. I usually go to the bank at 8. I get to the bank at 9.00 am. At 1.30 pm I go to a café for lunch. At 3 I go back to the bank. I go home at about 6. I get home at 6.45 pm. On Friday I usually go to the cinema in the evening.

8 2 Where do you work?
3 What time do you go to the bank?
4 What time do you get to the bank?
5 Where do you go for lunch?
6 What time do you go home?
7 What do you do on Friday evenings?

9 Breakfast: 7.30 am
Go to office: 8.00 am
Get to office: 8.30 am
Lunch: 1.00 pm
Go home: 6.00 pm
Spanish class: 7.30 pm
Back home: 9.00 or 9.30 pm

10 2 False 3 True 4 True 5 True 6 True

Unit 3

1 twenty-two, two, twenty, fifteen, sixty-one, fifty-nine, eleven, three thirty, eight, twelve thirty.

2 2 mother   5 uncle
   3 daughter   6 wife
   4 grandfather   7 boyfriend

3 2 She is Japanese.
   3 He has got two daughters.
   4 She is married.
   5 Her name is Eva.
   6 His wife's name is Joan.
   7 She has got Marie's book.
   8 Ahmet's sister is twenty-one.
   9 What is your father's name?

4 2 How many children has he got?
   3 How many great-great-grandchildren has he got?
   4 How many grandchildren has he got?

5 3 True.
   4 False. Carlos is Ramón's grandfather.
   5 True.
   6 True.
   7 False. Marta is Elvira's mother.
   8 False. Francisco and Isabella have got two children.
   9 True.
   10 False. Juan is Carlos' son.
   11 True.

6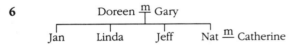

7 2 Jan is Gary's daughter.
   3 Catherine and Nat are married. (or: Nat and Catherine are married)
   4 Gary and Doreen are Nat's parents. (or: Nat's parents are Gary and Doreen).
   5 He has got one brother.
   6 Catherine and Nat haven't got any children.
   7 Nat is Jeff's brother. (or: Jeff's brother is Nat.)
   8 Jan has got two brothers.
   9 Gary and Doreen have got three children.

8 2 Who is Carlos?
   3 Have you got any sisters?
   4 Who is Marta?
   5 Is Francisco married?
   6 Who is Isabella?
   7 Have Francisco and Isabella got any children?

9 2 Whose is the orange juice? Monica's.
   3 Whose is the croissant? Dora's.
   4 Whose is the egg? Ken's.
   5 Whose is the toast? Christopher's.
   6 Whose is the coffee? Odile's.

Unit 4

1 2 Whose books are these?
   3 They're Alfonso's.
   4 These are Spanish wines.
   5 Are these your pens?
   6 They're Portuguese.
   7 Are your sisters married?
   8 Have these children got English books?
   9 These people are my friends.

2 1 skiing   7 climbing
   2 sailing   8 playing tennis
   3 exercising   9 horse-riding
   4 playing golf   10 playing basketball
   5 running   11 playing baseball
   6 swimming

3 2 I come from Brazil but I don't like listening to Brazilian music.
   3 I come from Greece but I don't like eating Greek food.
   4 She comes from Australia but she doesn't like drinking Australian beer.
   5 He comes from Spain but he doesn't like watching Spanish television.
   6 I come from Egypt but I don't like reading Egyptian magazines.
   7 We come from Portugal but we don't like drinking Portuguese wine.
   8 He comes from Holland but he doesn't like eating Dutch cheese.
   9 She comes from Switzerland but she doesn't like eating Swiss chocolates.

5 Her name is Carolien. She comes from Holland. She's 20 years old. She's got two brothers and a sister. Her sister's name is Hilda. Carolien's a student. She likes sports, television and reading.

6
1 2 She has breakfast at 7.30.
   3 She goes to the University at 8.30.
   4 She gets to the University at 9.00.
   5 She has lunch at 1.00.
   6 She goes shopping at 2.00.
   7 She gets home at 3.00.
   9 She studies.
   10 She watches television.
   11 She goes to bed at 12.00.

6
2 2 What time do you have breakfast?
   3 What time do you go to the University?
   4 What time do you get to the University?

6
3 2 What time does Carolien go shopping?
   3 What time does she get home?
   4 What time does she go to bed?

7 2 Carolien has breakfast at home but Hilda has breakfast at the University.
   3 Carolien has lunch at 1:00 but Hilda has lunch at 2.00.
   4 Carolien gets home at 3.00 but Hilda gets home at about 4.00.
   5 Carolien does the housework but Hilda cooks dinner.
   6 Carolien watches television but Hilda reads or listens to music.
   7 Carolien goes to bed at 12.00 but Hilda goes to bed at 1.00.

8 1d, 2g, 3a, 4f, 5c, 6b, 7e

9

	tea	coffee	beer	wine
Gül	✓	✓	✗	✗
Rosa	✗	✓	✗	✓
André	✓	✓	✓	✗
Leila	✓	✗	✗	✗

11 3 Different
  4 Same
  5 Same
  6 Different
  7 Different
  8 Different
  9 Same

Unit 5

1 2 Excuse me?/sorry.
  3 please?/Sorry/Thank you.
  4 Excuse me/Sorry
  5 Sorry

3 2 30
  3 15
  4 17, 19
  5 50
  6 6.15
  7 905 34 86
  8 9.45
  9 14, 12, 5, 40, 14

4
1 1 Is the shop open? Yes, it is.
  2 Where do you come from? Wales.
  3 Anything else? No, thank you.
  4 How do you spell that? W-A-L-E-S
  5 What's your name? Megan.
  6 How old are you? I'm 27.
  7 Can I have a bottle of milk? Here you are.
  8 Are you married? Yes, I am.
  9 Have you got any children? Yes, two boys.

2 Conversation one: 1, 7, 3
  Conversation two: 5, 2, 4, 8, 9

5 2 Thank you
  3 Sumimasen
  4 Ohayo gozaimasu
  5 Good afternoon

6
1 bye *infml* goodbye
  hi! *infml* hello
  ta *infml* thank you
  hey! a shout used to call attention or to express surprise, interest, etc.
  yeah *infml* yes

2 A: Excuse me!
  B: Yes?
  A: Have you got the time?
  B: It's 5.45.
  A: Thank you.
  B: Good bye.
  A: Good bye.

7

1	2	3	4	5
hey!	tea	I	know	two
they	we	hi!	no	do
say	three	bye		to
	me	buy		
	she			

8 Name: Debbie Cartwright.
  Address: 234 West Green Rd, London N4 OET
  Tel. No: 081 318 0122
  Country of origin: Canada
  Age: 34
  Marital Status: married
  No. of children: 2 daughters

9 lives/speaks/is/is/is/is/have got/like/listening

Unit 6

1
1 2 walk; 3 work; 4 wash; 5 listen; 6 cook; 7 dance
2 watched; walked; worked; washed; ; listened; cooked; danced.
3 washed, cooked, listened, walked, worked, watched, danced.
4 walked; bought; did; had; visited; watched; wrote; did; read; went.
5 2 Why did she buy cheese, ham and tomatoes?
  3 Why did she visit her parents?
  4 Why did they watch a video?
  5 Why did she write a long letter to her aunt?
  6 Why did she do her French homework?
  7 Why did she read a book?

2 1898 he was born
  1919 he made his first million
  1921 he visited the Soviet Union
  1923 he married Olga
  1931 he went back to USA
  1956 he started a petroleum business
  1990 he died

3 He was born in England in April 1564. He went to work in London. He was an actor and writer. His wife's name was Anne. He wrote 38 plays. He died in 1616.
Puzzle: William Shakespeare

4 2 He moved to Italy in 1569.
  3 He married Catalina in 1584.
  4 He wrote 16 plays.
  5 He wrote *Don Quixote* (Part 1) in 1605.
  6 He wrote *Don Quixote* (Part 2) in 1615.
  7 He died in 1616.
Puzzle: They both wrote plays. They both died in 1616.

5 Christopher Marlowe was an English poet and dramatist. He was born in Canterbury in 1564. His father was a shoemaker. He went to Cambridge University. He wrote *Doctor Faustus* in 1590. In 1593 he was killed in a fight in Deptford.
Puzzle: They were both born in 1564.

7 2 on; 3 in; 4 in; 5 on; 6 on; 7 in.

8 dentist: a person professionally trained to treat teeth
  teacher: a person who teaches, esp. as a profession
  pilot: a person who flies an aircraft
  soldier: a member of the army
  waiter: a person who serves food at the tables in a restaurant
  student: a person who is studying at a place of education or training
  politician: a person whose business is politics

9 2 his; 3 his; 4 my; 5 this/his; 6 these are her.

Unit 7

1 a 11; b 10; c 4; d 1; e 9; f 7; g 5; h 6; i 3; j 2; k 8

2 bars/ There's / There's / There are/ 's a/ There are/ There's a/ There's a/

3 2 False; 3 True; 4 False; 5 True; 6 False; 7 True.

	Greta	Brita	Wim
Month	July	August	June
City	Madrid	Cairo	Venice
Hotel	Ritz	Grand	Excelsior

6 2 Brita didn't stay in the Excelsior.
3 Greta didn't go to Madrid in June.
4 Wim didn't go to Madrid.
5 Brita didn't go to Cairo in July.
6 Greta didn't go to Venice.

7 2 our; 3 your; 4 his; 5 their; 6 our; 7 your; 8 their; 9 her

8 1 would you like; 2 they're; 3 his; 4 we like; 5 this; 6 do you like; 7 he's; 8 I like; 9 was; 10 these; 11 was.

9 2 Jianguo Hotel
3 Friendship Hotel
4 Lusongyuan Guest House
5 The Great Wall Hotel

10 Is there air conditioning in every room?
Is there a swimming pool?
Is there television in every room?
Is there a health club?
Are there rooms with private bathrooms?
How much is a double room with a private bathroom?

Unit 8

1 2 shirt; 3 sweater; 4 shoes; 5 dress; 6 trousers; 7 shorts; 8 tights; 9 pyjamas.

2 1 1C; 2A; 3B;
2 1 £6.99; 2 white; 3 from all good casual clothing shops

3 2 father's car; 3 Charles/started/March; 4 aunt can't dance; 5 Martha/aren't/France; 6 bar/car park; 7 card.

4 2 I haven't got a car.
3 She can't speak German.
4 They aren't brothers.
5 Eric hasn't got a video.
6 We don't like playing football.
7 They don't live in London.
8 Virginia doesn't work in a bank.
9 I don't smoke.

5 a book

6 2 She's going to see Tosca on Monday.
3 She's going to dance on Tuesday.
4 She's going to have dinner (with Alfredo) on Wednesday.
5 She's going to stay at the Hotel Akropolis (on the 20th and 21st of June).
6 She's going to buy a villa (in Mykonos).
7 She's going to meet her bank manager (on Friday 21st).

7 Yes, I am.
I'm going to dance.
Where are you going to dance?
At the Teatro Bellini.
I'm going to fly to Athens.
What are you going to do in Athens?
I'm going to meet my bank manager.
Why are you going to meet your bank manager?

8 Constantin's letter is more formal.

10 2 No, it isn't.
3 Yes, I am.
4 Yes, I can.
5 Yes, it has.
6 Yes, I did.
7 Yes, I am.
8 No, it doesn't.
9 No, it isn't.

11 A bat.

Unit 9

1 2 I drove a car.
3 Did she speak Hindi?
4 He read Arabic.
5 I put the film in the camera.
6 Did you like the play?
7 They didn't go to school.
8 Did he smoke?
9 Anna wrote music and Ben played it.

3 1 Open your mouth; 2 Move your foot; 3 Clean your teeth; 4 Wash your face; 5 Touch your toes.

4
1 2

2 2 Lift your left knee
3 Pull your knee down.
4 Stretch your right leg.
5 Now lift your right knee.
6 Pull your knee down and stretch your left leg.

3 4

5 2 X is on Y
3 Z is in O
4 D is behind C
5 J is in front of K
6 V is on the right of U
7 V is on the left of W
8 M is under L
9 F is above G

6 From left to right: Aunt Vera, Annie's father, Annie, Eddie, Sylvia, Uncle Jack

7 1 shoe; 2 shut; 3 hair; 4 right; 5 suit; 6 knee; 7 move; 8 five.

8 2 Can you speak Portuguese?
No, I can't. But I can understand Portuguese.
3 Can you play squash?
No, I can't. But I can play tennis.
4 Can you drive a bus?
No, I can't. But I can drive a car.
5 Can you dance?
No, I can't. But I can sing.
6 Can you play the guitar?
No, I can't. But I can play the piano.

7 Can you use a computer?
No, I can't. But I can use a calculator.

9 2 can; 3 can; 4 can't; 5 can; 6 can't; 7 can; 8 can; 9 can't.

10 2 Don't talk. 3 Don't take photographs. 4 Don't touch the exhibits. 5 Don't walk on the grass. 6 Don't eat or drink. 7 Don't park. 8. Don't play ball games. 9. Don't dance or sing.

Unit 10

1 1e; 2h; 3f; 4a; 5j; 6d; 7i; 8g; 9c; 10b

2
1 2 2; 3 3; 4 2; 5 2; 6 1; 7 4; 8 3; 9 1
2 2 fifteenth; 3 July; 4 hamburger; 5 ice-cream; 6 perfume; 7 magazine; 8 Chinese; 9 receptionist.

3 2 boys; 3 babies; 4 families; 5 men; 6 women; 7 children; 8 people; 9 feet.

4 1c; 2b; 3d; 4c

6
1 1 5; 2 Bob, Anna, Claude, Martin, Gianella.
2 1 Bob; 2 Martin; 3 Claude; 4 Anna; 5 Gianella.

8 on; music; started; graduated; met; studying; teacher; from; wrote; in; died.

9 My brother (or me)

Unit 11

1
1 religion/religious; intelligence/intelligent; affection/affectionate; politics/political; sincerity/sincere; attraction/attractive; stupidity/stupid; humour/humorous; love/lovely; beauty/beautiful; profession/professional
2 2 politics; 3 religion; 4 intelligent; 5 humour.

2 is; is; has got; are; is; has got; is; is; has got; is; is; has got.

3
1 brown eyes, short, dark hair, good looking
2 sincere, kind
3 not very affectionate, beautiful, not very intelligent, not very attractive

4 Paragraph 1
The first time I met Celia we were both students. She was eighteen and I was twenty-one. I liked her immediately. But she wasn't interested.
Paragraph 2
The second time we met was five years later. It was my twenty-sixth birthday party. This time she was interested, but I was married.
Paragraph 3
Five years later we met again. My marriage was finished and I was lonely. But she was a happily married twenty-eight year old, with two children. I wonder when we'll meet again?

5 2 She's married to him; 3 He likes her; 4 She lives with him; 5 He works with them; 6 They play tennis with them; 7 She meets him; 8 He works with him.

6 2 When did Eleanor meet Gary?
She met him ___ years ago.
3 When did Rita and her husband part?
They parted ___ years ago.
4 When did Joe meet Rita?
He met her ___ months ago.
5 When did Gary go on holiday?
He went on holiday one month ago.
6 When did Gary come home?
He came home two days ago.

7 2 unstressed; 3 stressed; 4 unstressed; 5 stressed; 6 stressed; 7 unstressed; 8 unstressed; 9 stressed.

8 b

9 2 was; 3 were; 4 were; 5 was; 6 were; 7 was; 8 were; 9 were.

11 a Separate futures, please.
b Business is terrible.
c Go quickly, my husband is coming.

Unit 12

1 underground, taxi, train, boat, bicycle, bus.

2 Uncountable: olive oil, sugar, juice, water, stuffing, garlic, parsley, salt.
Countable: aubergines, ingredients, lemon, onions, tomatoes.

3 yes: sugar, salt, garlic.
no: aubergines, olive oil, onions, tomatoes, lemons, parsley.

4 3 They haven't got any olive oil.
4 They've got some salt.
5 They haven't got any onions.
6 They haven't got any tomatoes.
7 They haven't got any lemons.
8 They've got some garlic.
9 They haven't got any parsley.

5 1d; 2f; 3g; 4i; 5a; 6e; 7h; 8c; 9j; 10b

6 3 them; 4 them; 5 it; 6 it; 7 it; 8 them; 9 it; 10 it.

7 2 unstressed; 3 stressed; 4 stressed; 5 unstressed; 6 unstressed; 7 stressed.

9 1 next to; 2 a long way from; 3 near (or not far from); 4 not far from (or near).

10 1b
2

vegetables	meat	fish	herbs	dried fruit	others
onions tomatoes red peppers	rabbit pork lamb	cod shellfish	oregano rosemary thyme bay leaves	raisins prunes	olive oil nuts garlic

Unit 13

1 1 1 rain; 2 sun; 3 cloud; 4 wind; 5 snow; 6 fog.
2 2 mist; 3 breeze; 4 hail; 5 ice; 6 thunderstorm.
3 2 sunny; 3 cloudy; 4 foggy; 5 showery; 6 stormy; 7 icy; 8 windy.

2 Wind symbol on Newfoundland coast, snow symbol on Québec, fog symbol on Ontario, cloud symbol on Manitoba and Saskatchewan, rain symbol on Lake Winnipeg, sun symbol on British Columbia, fog symbol on Vancouver.

3

1
2 What's the weather like in Bahrain today?
   It's dry.
3 What's the weather like in Cairo today?
   It's sunny.
4 What's the weather like in Chicago today?
   It's snowing.
5 What's the weather like in Bangkok today?
   It's cloudy.
6 What's the weather like in Bombay today?
   It's raining.
7 What's the weather like in Amsterdam today?
   It's foggy.

2
2 What's the weather like?
3 What are your brothers like?
4 What's the English language like?
5 What's her sister like?
6 What are snails like?
7 What's your flat like?
8 What are Buddy Holly's songs like?

4 2 3; 3 8; 4 2; 5 5; 6 1; 7 6; 8 4

5
2 Is it raining?
3 What is your brother doing?
4 Are you wearing a white T-shirt?
5 Why is she wearing her red shoes?
6 Why are you doing this exercise?

6 Bodmin; comfortable; delicious; friendly; sitting; hot; reading; playing; wearing; like; raining

7 2 unfinished; 3 finished; 4 unfinished; 5 finished; 6 unfinished; 7 finished; 8 unfinished; 9 unfinished; 10 finished.

9 blizzard: a long severe snowstorm
mess: a state of disorder and untidiness
chaos: a state of complete disorder and confusion
traffic jam: a mass of vehicles so close together that movement is difficult or impossible
disaster: a sudden great misfortune
crash: to (cause to) have a violent and noisy accident

10 2 True; 3 True; 4 False; 5 False; 6 False

11 2 It; 3 it; 4 She; 5 It; 6 it; 7 they; 8 They; 9 him

Unit 14

1

	Size	Appearance	Health	Character	Age
1	tall	attractive	healthy	clever	old
	big	dark	tired	friendly	young
	heavy	dirty	ill	intelligent	
	short	fair	well	boring	
2	taller	more attractive	healthier	cleverer	older
	bigger	darker	more tired	friendlier	younger
	heavier	dirtier	iller	more intelligent	
	shorter	fairer	better	more boring	

2
2 Tom is bigger than Dick.
3 Dick is happier than Tom.
4 Dick is more intelligent than Tom.
5 Tom is dirtier than Dick.
6 Dick is healthier than Tom.
7 Tom is heavier than Dick.
8 Tom is taller than Dick.
9 Dick is more attractive than Tom.
10 Dick is shorter than Tom.

3 bigger; hotter; prettier; better; tidier; happier; drier; sunnier; wetter; sadder.

5
2 What do you do?
3 Where do you live?
4 Where do you live?
5 What would you like?
6 What would you like?
7 Are you married?
8 Are you married?
9 What's your flat like?
10 What's your flat like?

7 c

8 2 should; 3 shouldn't; 4 should; 5 shouldn't; 6 should; 7 shouldn't; 8 shouldn't; 9 should; 10 should.

9 2 has got; 3 is; 4 have got; 5 am; 6 Are; 7 is; 8 is, has got.

10 1 head; 2 throat; 3 chest; 4 back; 5 arm; 6 leg; 7 brain; 8 heart; 9 lungs; 10 liver; 11 stomach.

11 There are problems in the man's liver, back and head.

Unit 15

1

	1	2	3	4
	marriage	aunt	sausages	witch
	funeral	uncle	turkey	ghost
	birthday	cousin	sweets	monster

2
Happy birthday! — Thank you.
I love you! — I love you, too.
Happy New Year! — You too!
Good luck! — I'll need it!
Thanks for a great party. — I'm glad you could come.
I'm sorry. — That's all right.
Congratulations! — Thank you.
Good bye. — See you soon.

3 2 c; 3 b; 4 a; 5 b; 6 c; 7 b; 8 a; 9 b.

4
1 Diwali is one of the most important Hindu festivals. It is celebrated in honour of Lakshmi, the Goddess of wealth. It lasts three days and is celebrated in October or November. Traditionally, Hindus eat lots of sweets, exchange presents, and light fires during the festival. They also put lights in the doors of their houses (Diwali means 'little lights').
2 Thanksgiving Day is celebrated in the United States on the fourth Thursday in November. It was first celebrated in 1621 to thank God for a good harvest. Traditionally, families have a Thanksgiving dinner where they eat turkey and pumpkin pie.

2
1 In honour of Lakshmi.
2 In October or November.
3 Three days.
4 They eat lots of sweets, exchange presents, light fires, and put lights in the doors of their houses.
5 Lots of sweets.

3 1 Why is Thanksgiving celebrated?
To thank God for a good harvest.
2 When is it celebrated?
On the fourth Thursday in November.
3 How long does Thanksgiving last?
One day.
4 What do Americans do on Thanksgiving?
They have a Thanksgiving dinner.
5 What do they eat?
They eat turkey and pumpkin pie.

5 2 in; 3 was; 4 had; 5 the; 6 were; 7 and; 8 were; 9 it; 10 we; 11 by; 12 is; 13 from; 14 a; 15 more; 16 in; 17 have; 18 hotter; 19 was; 20 are; 21 staying; 22 the; 23 more; 24 than.

6
1 Cuba
2 f, b, c, d, a, e

Unit 16

1 expensive cheap; high low; comfortable uncomfortable; rich poor; safe dangerous; fast slow; difficult easy; narrow wide; interesting boring; heavy light.

2
1 2 the safest; 3 the richest; 4 most expensive; 5 the most difficult; 6 the most interesting; 7 the most dangerous; 8 the heaviest
2 2 What is the longest river in South America?
3 What are the highest falls in South America (or the world)?
4 What is the most southerly point in South America?
5 What is the largest lake in South America?
6 What is the deepest depression in South America?

3 1 Rio, Ascunción, Corumba, La Paz, Machupicchu, Lima; 1 Rio; 2 The train journey to Bolivia; 3 Machupicchu.

4
1 1 The train; 2 The bus; 3 The train.
2 E

5 turn, Walk, reach, left, Take, first, along, left.

6 2 finished; 3 finished; 4 unfinished; 5 unfinished; 6 finished.

8 Dear Chris,
How are you? I'm glad that you can come and visit us next weekend. My brother and his girlfriend are coming too, but there are lots of beds. And we have a tent, too, if the weather stays warm. / The best way to get here is to take the Holyhead train from Euston Station and get out at Conway. You may have to change at Crewe. We'll meet you at the station. / How was your trip to South America? Did you take lots of photos? You can tell us all about it when you come. / Well, that's all for now. See you on Saturday.
   Best wishes,
   Mark.

Unit 17

1 Across 1 SRI LANKA; 2 UGANDA; 3 PAKISTAN; 4 MALTA; 5 CYPRUS; 6 JAMAICA; 7 IRELAND; 8 FIJI; 9 CANADA;
Down 10 AUSTRALIA

2 1 the; – ; a; the; The; – ; the; the.

2

3
1 Australia, New Zealand, Singapore, Hong Kong, Fiji, Hawaii, Los Angeles, San Francisco.
2 Has Russell been to Singapore? Yes, he has.
Has Russell been to Tahiti? Yes, he has.
Has Russell been to Indonesia? I don't know.
Has Russell been to Japan? I don't know.
Has Russell been to the United States? Yes, he has.
Has Russell been to Thailand? Yes, he has.
Has Russell been to Beijing? I don't know

4 YOU: Is that Russell?
RUSSELL: Yes, it is
YOU: Have you ever been to Tasmania?
RUSSELL: Yes, I have.
YOU: Where is it?
RUSSELL: It's south of Australia.
YOU: What's the capital?
RUSSELL: Hobart
YOU: When did you go there?
RUSSELL: Last year.
YOU: What's it like?
RUSSELL: It's beautiful. Really lovely.
YOU: Are there any good hotels?
RUSSELL: Yes, lots of very good hotels.
YOU: Are there any national parks?
RUSSELL: Yes, there are.
YOU: Well, thanks a lot, Russell. You've been very helpful.
RUSSELL: You're welcome. (Not at all.)
YOU: Bye.

6 1 Peter Conrad; 2 Down Home; 3 Non-fiction; 4 Tasmania (Australia); 5 Yes; 6 In 1968; 7 £5.99

7

Country	When visited	Opinion
China	recently	fascinating
Antarctica	1987	interesting, cold
Burma	1966	dangerous
Tasmania	next month	–

8 2 She's been to Egypt.
3 She's worked in the Middle East
4 She's lived in Ireland.
5 She's written a book/books.

9 4, 7, 5, 3, 8, 2, 1, 6.

10 2 I've been to China a number of times.
3 But I've never written a book about it.
4 I've only ever been there once.
5 Is there anywhere you haven't been?

11 Tasmania is a state of Australia, consisting of one large island and several smaller islands situated south-east of the continent of Australia. The capital of Tasmania is Hobart, in the south, with a population of 127,000.

Unit 18

1
Across	Down
1 SHIRT	1 SOCK
5 SKIRT	2 TIE
6 BOOT	3 PULLOVER
7 BLOUSE	4 TROUSERS
8 SWEATER	6 BELT
9 SHORTS	8 SHOES
11 SUIT	10 HAT

2
1. Can you watch the dog, please?
2. Do you like chips?
3. Can you cash this for me?
4. What would you like? New shoes
5. Are those animals sheep?
6. Would you like a cherry?
7. I'm looking for the shops.

3

1 2 sister-in-law; 3 niece; 4 great-aunt; 5 stepdaughter; 6 granddaughter

2 2 cousin; 3 great-uncle; 4 stepson; 5 nephew; 6 brother-in-law

4 1

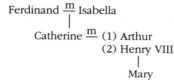

2 d

5 2 carefully; 3 well; 4 fast; 5 quick; 6 politely; 7 good; 8 lightly.

7 1 c; 2 e; 3 g; 4 a; 5 f; 6 d; 7 b

8 2 too/very; 3 too; 4 very; 5 very; 6 very.

9

1 2 Do you have to travel a lot?
3 Do you have to use your hands?
4 Do you have to speak in public?
5 Do you have to work at night?
6 Do you have to wear a crown?
7 Are you a king/queen/prince/princess?

2 2 Queens don't have to take public transport.
3 A king doesn't have to pay rent.
4 Kings and queens don't have to have a passport.
5 The Queen doesn't have to cook.
6 Princes and princesses don't have to work.
7 Kings and queens don't have to drive.

Unit 19

1 got married; got worse; got better; got tired; got divorced; got older

2 2 Do; 3 will; 4 did; 5 will; 6 do; 7 will; 8 Did; 9 do; 10 Will.

3 2 Different; 3 Different; 4 Same; 5 Different; 6 Different; 7 Same.

4 10

6
Down	Across
1 WATER	3 HEATED
2 VIDEO	5 BEDROOM
4 CUPBOARD	9 PATIO
5 BATH	10 FLAT
6 DOOR	12 APARTMENTS
7 OFFICE	14 DOWNSTAIRS
8 STEPS	
11 IRON	
13 MAT	

7 d

8 a 7; b 2; c 8; d 3; e 5; f 1; g 6; h 4.

Unit 20

1 library; sofa; French; examination.

2 2 chemistry   7 arithmetic
3 biology   8 university
4 examinations 9 library
5 geography   10 education
6 mathematics

4 1 Reading: Tessa reads fiction and non-fiction with fluency.
Writing: She is an imaginative story-writer. Her spelling and punctuation is good.
Oral commmunication: She is a good listener and a good speaker and she participates in class discussions.
Mathematics: Works hard but she is not good at numbers.
Science: Tessa is an enthusiastic researcher and has done excellent projects.
Physical education: Tessa enjoys games and gymnastics.
Art/music/drama: Tessa is a member of the school choir and she enjoys painting.

2 1 no; 2 yes; 3 OK; 4 yes; 5 usual, write, writing, probably, recess, teacher, writes.

5 2 She doesn't like maths.
3 Her grammar is better than her spelling.
4 Why don't you like music?
5 He writes English very well.
6 We haven't got any books.
7 What is Tessa doing?
8 She is practising her spelling.

6
8.15	Teacher gets to work
9.15–9.45	Reading
9.45–11.00	Maths
11.00–12.30	Science/Arts (Practical) Maths
12.30	Lunch
2.45	Games/PE
3.45	Children go home
5.30	Teacher goes home

8 1 1898; 2 1616; 3 arigato gozaimasu; 4 3 Hai Dian Road; 5 In October or November; 6 12,500,00; 7 12,000 square miles; 8 70; 9 The United States; 10 1926; 11 Cerro Aconcagua; 12 40 miles; 13 Mary I; 14 Hobart; 15 Peter Conrad.

3 Grammar: *What's it like*

1 Look at the weather for today. Write questions and answers.

WORLD WEATHER
Yesterday, Midday: c. cloud; dr. dry; f. fair; fg. fog; r. rain; sn. snow; s. sunny

	C		C
Ajaccio	s 25	Berlin	c 22
Algiers	c 28	Bombay	r 34
Amsterdam	fg 17	Buenos Aires	s 16
Athens	s 30	Cairo	s 33
Bahrain	dr 34	Chicago	sn 3
Bangkok	c 32	Dhahran	c 38
Barbados	c 32	Dubrovnik	s 24
Barcelona	c 28	Florence	s 27

1 What's *the weather like in* Berlin *today*?
It's *cloudy*.
2 What _____ Bahrain _____?
It _____
3 _____ Cairo _____?
It _____
4 _____ Chicago _____?
_____
5 _____ Bangkok _____?
_____
6 _____ Bombay _____?
_____
7 _____ Amsterdam _____?
_____

2 Make questions using *to be* + *like*.

1 (Toronto) *What's Toronto like?*
2 (the weather) _____?
3 (your brothers) _____?
4 (the English language) _____?
5 (her sister) _____?
6 (snails) _____?
7 (your flat) _____?
8 (Buddy Holly's songs) _____?

4 Vocabulary

Now match these answers to the questions in Exercise 3:2.

1 It's big and sunny. **7**
2 They're tall. ___
3 They're sad. ___
4 It's hot and stormy. ___
5 She's pretty. ___
6 It's big and crowded. ___
7 They're delicious. ___
8 It's easy. ___

5 Grammar: Present Continuous

Put the words in the correct order to make questions.

1 wearing they are what?
What are they wearing?
2 raining it is?
_____
3 brother what doing your is?
_____
4 T-shirt you are white wearing a?
_____
5 her why she shoes wearing red is?
_____
6 doing you are why exercise this?
_____

6 Writing

Complete the postcard using these words.

like friendly hot raining sitting wearing
comfortable playing reading Bodmin delicious

Dear Gabriella,
Here we are in _____. It's really very nice here. The hotel is _____ and the food is _____. The people in the village are very _____. I'm _____ in the garden of the hotel at the moment and the weather is lovely. It's _____ and sunny. Philip is _____ the newspaper and the children are _____ by the pool. Ellen is _____ the green sun hat you gave her. How are you all? What is the weather _____ there? Is it _____?
See you soon,
love Ann.

7 Pronunciation: intonation

Listen to the cassette. Decide if the descriptions are *finished* or *unfinished*.

1 The sun is shining ___*unfinished*___
2 The birds are singing _____
3 I'm sitting in the garden _____
4 The children are playing _____
5 Philip is reading a book _____
6 A woman is walking into the bank _____
7 She's wearing a green dress _____
8 She's wearing a grey jacket _____
9 She's carrying an umbrella _____
10 She's leaving the bank _____

8 Speaking

Listen to the cassette and respond to the questions.

Example:
CASSETTE: Hello. How are you? What's that noise? It sounds like a party. Are you two having a party?
YOU: No, we're not having a party exactly.

9 Dictionary work

Match the words with the dictionary definitions.

- blizzard
- mess
- chaos
- traffic jam
- disaster
- crash

- a sudden great misfortune
- a mass of vehicles so close together that movement is difficult or impossible
- a long severe snowstorm
- to (cause to) have a violent and noisy accident
- a state of complete disorder and confusion
- a state of disorder or untidiness; dirty material

10 Reading

Read the newspaper article and decide if these sentences are *True* or *False*.

1 It snowed last night. ___*True*___
2 More snow is coming. _____
3 The worst weather was in Kent and Essex. _____
4 Southend had 2 inches of snow in 8 hours. _____
5 The trains are running normally. _____
6 Most major roads are closed. _____

It's going to get worse!

LONDON is expecting another foot of snow this weekend. The blizzards which paralysed the South-east are going to get worse.

A London Weather Centre spokesman said: 'There was nearly a foot of snow last night in some places in the South-east and there may be another foot in the next 48 hours.'

'Kent and Essex have caught the worst. We have had reports from Southend of eight inches of snow in two hours.'

On the railways, there was total chaos. British Rail admits that 'We're in a mess.' Most major roads are open, but motorists are experiencing traffic jams and long delays getting home.

From the Evening Standard

11 Grammar: pronouns

Complete the sentences with the correct pronoun.

1 Do you like my shoes? Yes, I like ___*them*___ a lot.
2 What's the weather like? _____'s raining.
3 Do you like my car? Yes, _____'s nice.
4 What's Ellen like? _____'s nice.
5 What's the time? _____'s five o'clock.
6 How long does _____ take to get to Birmingham? Two hours.
7 Do you like her clothes? Yes, _____'re OK.
8 What are his books like? _____'re interesting.
9 Do you like Buddy Holly? Yes, I like _____ a lot.

Unit 14

1 Vocabulary: adjectives

Write the adjectives in the correct category (size, appearance, health, character, age) in box 1. Write the comparative form of the adjectives in box 2.

healthy tall friendly
attractive well intelligent
big clever dark heavy
old dirty boring tired
fair ill short young

	size	appearance	health	character	age
1				clever	
2				cleverer	

2 Grammar: comparative adjectives

Look at the pictures. Write sentences comparing Tom and Dick.

1 (old) *Tom is older than Dick.*
2 (big)
3 (happy)
4 (intelligent)
5 (dirty)
6 (healthy)
7 (heavy)
8 (tall)
9 (attractive)
10 (short)

Tom   Dick

3 Spelling

There are ten spelling mistakes in the text. Find them and correct them.

Paris is my favourite city. New York is biger, and Rome is hoter, but Paris is prettyer. The food is beter, too. And the streets are cleaner and tidyer. People are happyer in Paris, I think. Perhaps because the weather is dryer and sunnyer. London is weter than Paris and the people are sader.

4 Writing

○ Write ten sentences comparing cities you know.

1 Paris is more beautiful than …
2 ___
3 ___
4 ___
5 ___
6 ___
7 ___
8 ___
9 ___
10 ___

5 Pronunciation: sentence stress

Listen to the cassette and mark the stressed words in these sentences.

1 What do you do?
2 What do you do?
3 Where do you live?
4 Where do you live?
5 What would you like?
6 What would you like?
7 Are you married?
8 Are you married?
9 What's your flat like?
10 What's your flat like?

6 Speaking

Listen to the cassette. Respond and return the questions.

Example:
CASSETTE: What do you do?
YOU: (doctor) I'm a doctor. What *you* do?

1 doctor   4 French   7 yes
2 Brighton   5 yes   8 red wine
3 Bristol   6 no

7 Reading

Read the letter to a magazine and decide which picture is 'Max'.

Dear Deborah …

My problem is that I can't stop smoking. I started smoking 3 years ago. I live with my parents. My father smokes but my mother doesn't. They both want me to stop smoking. They say I can't smoke in the house. Do you think I should leave home? My teacher gets angry if I smoke at school. I want to leave school and get a job where I can smoke. I tried to stop once, but it was impossible. Do you think I should see a doctor?
Yours, Max

a
b
c
d

8 Grammar: should/shouldn't

Complete the advice that Deborah gives to Max in Exercise 7, using should or shouldn't.

1 I agree with your parents. You **shouldn't** smoke.
2 You _____ give up smoking.
3 You _____ smoke in the house.
4 Your father _____ stop smoking, too.
5 No, you _____ leave home.
6 You _____ listen to your teacher.
7 You _____ smoke at school.
8 You _____ leave school.
9 You _____ stop smoking again.
10 Yes, I think you _____ see a doctor.

9 Grammar: have got/to be

Complete the sentences with the correct form of to be or have got in the present tense.

1 I **am** not very well.
2 She _____ a toothache.
3 Close the door. It _____ cold.
4 What's the matter? I _____ a cold.
5 How old are you? I _____ twenty-five.
6 _____ you hungry?
7 How _____ your daughter?
8 She _____ tired. She _____ a stomachache.

10 Vocabulary: parts of the body

Write the names next to the correct parts of the body.

arm   head   leg   throat   back   chest   lungs   heart
brain   stomach   liver

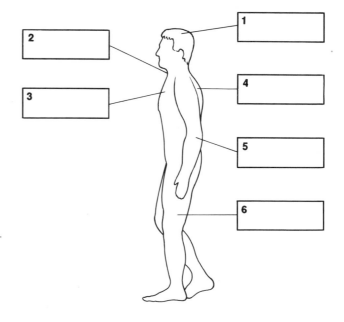

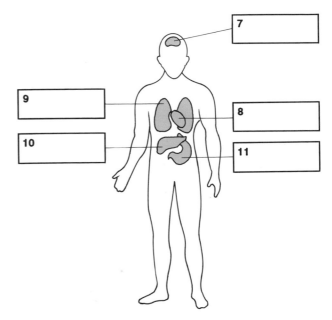

11 Listening

🔊 Listen to the conversation and mark on the pictures in Exercise 10 where there is a problem.

Unit 15

1 Vocabulary: celebrations

1 Put the following words into four groups. There should be three words in each group.

marriage   aunt   sweets
sausages   ghost   uncle
witch   funeral cousin
turkey   monster birthday

1	2	3	4
marriage	aunt		

2 Now, add one more word to each group.

2 Conversation

Match the expressions on the left with the responses on the right.

1 Happy birthday!   See you soon.
2 I love you!   I'm glad you could
                             come.
3 Happy New Year!   Thank you.
4 Good luck!   I love you, too.
5 Thanks for a great party. That's all right.
6 I'm sorry.   Thank you.
7 Congratulations!   I'll need it!
8 Good bye.   You too!

3 Pronunciation: intonation

Listen to the cassette and decide which picture matches each example.

1 Thank you. _a_
2 Thank you. ____
3 Thank you. ____
4 Hello. ____
5 Hello. ____
6 Happy New Year. ____
7 Happy New Year. ____
8 Congratulations. ____
9 Congratulations. ____

4 Reading and writing

1 Separate these two texts about two festivals. Write the two texts below.

> **Diwali and Thanksgiving**
> Diwali is one of the most important Hindu festivals. Thanksgiving Day is celebrated in the United States on the fourth Thursday in November. It is celebrated in honour of Lakshmi, the Goddess of wealth. It lasts three days and is celebrated in October or November. It was first celebrated in 1621 to thank God for a good harvest. Traditionally, families have a Thanksgiving dinner where they eat turkey and pumpkin pie. Traditionally Hindus eat lots of sweets, exchange presents, and light fireworks during the festival. They also put lights in the doors of their houses (Diwali means 'little lights').

1 Diwali

2 Thanksgiving

2 Answer the questions about Diwali.

1 Why is Diwali celebrated?

2 When is it celebrated?

3 How long does Diwali last?

4 What do Hindus do on Diwali?

5 What do they eat?

3 Make similar questions for Thanksgiving, and write the answers.

1 *Why is* _____?

2 _____?

3 _____?

4 _____?

5 _____?

5 Grammar: review

Complete the letter with one word in each space.

Dear Ioanna,

Here we are in India! We got here (1) *on* Monday. We stayed (2)_____ Bombay for three days. It (3)_____ very hot but the hotel (4)_____ air conditioning. It was (5)_____ festival of Diwali. The streets (6)_____ crowded and there were fireworks (7)_____ lights and all the shops (8)_____ open: (9)_____ was fantastic. After Bombay (10)_____ went to Goa. We travelled (11)_____ train. Goa (12)_____ a long way (13)_____ Bombay. We stayed in (14)_____ hotel by the beach. It was (15)_____ expensive than the hotel (16)_____ Bombay, but it didn't (17)_____ air conditioning, and the weather was (18)_____ than in Bombay. It (19)_____ awful. Now we (20)_____ in Madras. We are (21)_____ in a very nice hotel near (22)_____ central railway station. I like Madras: it is (23)_____ interesting than Goa. And it is smaller (24)_____ Bombay. Well, that's all for now. Love to everyone.

  Isabel.

6 Listening

1 🎧 Listen to the description of a festival and answer the question.

In what country does the festival take place?

2 🎧 Now listen to the description again and put these sentences in the correct order.

a People drink a lot of beer. ____
b People go to the town square. ____
c The President makes a speech. _1_
d The music starts. ____
e People have a large dinner. ____
f Schools and offices close. ____

7 Writing

○ **Write about a traditional festival in your country. Before you start, think about these questions.**

Why is it celebrated?
When is it celebrated?
What do people do, traditionally?

Unit 16

1 Vocabulary: adjectives

Match each adjective in column A with its opposite in column B.

A	B
expensive	dangerous
high	wide
comfortable	slow
rich	light
safe	cheap
fast	poor
difficult	low
narrow	boring
interesting	easy
heavy	uncomfortable

2 Grammar: superlatives

1 Complete the sentences using superlatives of these adjectives.

interesting   rich   difficult   heavy   high
expensive   safe   dangerous

1 Ben Nevis is ___the highest___ mountain in the British Isles.
2 Flying is _____ way to travel.
3 Queen Elizabeth is _____ woman in the world: she's got millions of pounds.
4 The world's _____ painting is a Van Gogh: it cost millions of dollars.
5 Which is _____ language: Chinese, Russian or Arabic?
6 I like her: she is one of _____ people I know.
7 The motorbike is _____ form of transport: there are hundreds of accidents every year.
8 Lead is one of _____ metals.

2 Look at the map. Then write the questions for these answers.

1 Cerro Aconcagua.
   What is the highest mountain in South America?

2 The Amazon.
   _____

3 The Angel Falls.
   _____

4 Cape Horn.
   _____

5 Lago Titicaca
   _____

6 Salinas Grandes
   _____

Discovered in 1935 the Angel Falls in the Roraima Mountains are highest in the world. The total fall is 980 m. with the greatest single drop of 805 m.

South America's largest lake is Lago Titicaca, 8,030 km². Situated at 3,812 m. above sea level it is one of the world's highest bodies of water.

South America's highest mountain, Cerro Aconcagua, reaches 6,959 m. above sea level.

The deepest depression in South America is Salinas Grande on Peninsula Valdes, 40 m. below sea level.

Most southerly point in South America is Cape Horn at 55° 59's. latitude.

The Amazon is the longest river in South America (6,570 km. from source to mouth) and is the world's second longest. The drainage basin is the largest in the world and covers 7.05 million km² and the river flow is greater than any other (120,000 m³/second).

49

3 Listening

1 📼 Listen to Justine Woodley and draw a line on the map to show where she went.

2 📼 Listen again, and answer the questions.

1 Which city was the most expensive?

2 What was the worst thing that happened?

3 What was the most interesting place she visited?

4 Reading

1 Read the text below and answer the questions.

You are arriving at Heathrow Airport and going to the University of Reading. Which is the best way to get there?

1 Which is faster: the train or the bus?

2 Which is cheaper?

3 Which is more frequent?

GETTING TO THE UNIVERSITY

Reading is the county town of the Royal County of Berkshire, at the confluence of the Thames and Kennet, roughly forty miles west of London. It is a thriving centre of commerce and industry, and one of the best shopping centres in the south of England.

Fast trains run frequently to and from London (Paddington), the fastest taking only 22 minutes. An express bus service to London passes the University, and although slower and less frequent than the train it is considerably cheaper. London Airport (Heathrow) is served by a frequent direct bus service from Reading Station, with a journey time of 50 minutes. The University lies between the town and the M4 motorway.

From the *Postgraduate Prospectus of the University of Reading*

2 Look at the map and follow the directions. Decide which is Wessex Hall. A, B, C, D, E, or F?

If you arrive at Reading Station, take the bus to the University (Number 8) and get out at the Queen's Drive gate. Walk along Redlands Road and take the second road on your right (Upper Redlands Rd). Continue along this road until you reach Whiteknights Road. Wessex Hall is the first hall on your right after the lake. Alternatively, coming from Earley Station...

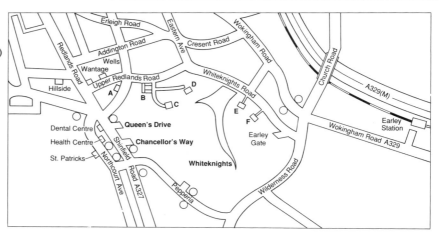

5 Grammar: street directions

Look at the map in Exercise 4:2 and complete the directions from Earley Station to Wessex Hall with these words:

along   left   left   first   get   turn   walk   take   reach

Take the train and **get** out at Earley Station. Walk until you reach Wokingham Road and _____ right. _____ along Wokingham Road until you _____ Wilderness Road. Turn _____. _____ the _____ road on the right. Go _____ this road, past Bridges Hall. Wessex Hall is the next hall on the _____.

6 Pronunciation: intonation

🔲 **Listen to the cassette and decide if the directions are finished or unfinished.**

1 *unfinished*
2 _____
3 _____
4 _____
5 _____
6 _____

7 Speaking

🔲 **Listen to the cassette and respond.**

Example:
CASSETTE: I think this one is the nicest.
YOU: I agree. But this one is nice, too.

8 Writing

Divide this letter into four paragraphs. Draw a line between each paragraph. One paragraph is done for you

Dear Chris,
How are you? I'm glad that you can come and visit us next weekend. My brother and his girlfriend are coming too, but there are lots of beds. And we have a tent, too, if the weather stays warm. The best way to get here is to take the Holyhead train from Euston Station and get out at Conway. You may have to change at Crewe. We'll meet you at the station. How was your trip to South America? Did you take lots of photos? You can tell us all about it when you come. / Well, that's all for now. See you on Saturday.

            Best wishes,
              Mark.

Unit 17

1 Vocabulary: countries

Complete the crossword.

Clue: These are all places in the English-speaking world.

Across
1 A country to the south of India.
2 A country in east Africa.
3 A country to the west of India.
4 An island in the central Mediterranean.
5 An island in the east Mediterranean.
6 An island in the Caribbean.
7 A country to the west of Great Britain.
8 A group of islands in the South Pacific.
9 A country in North America.

Down
10 An English-speaking country.

2 Grammar: articles

1 Complete the text with *a*, *the*, or leave the space blank if no article is necessary.

Tasmania is __*a*__ state of _____ Commonwealth of _____ Australia, consisting of _____ large island and several smaller islands south-east of _____ continent. _____ capital is _____ Hobart, which is in _____ south-east of _____ island.

2 Read the text about Tasmania and mark the underlined places on the map.

> The second largest city is Launceston in the north, which is connected to Hobart by road and rail. The most northerly point of the island is Cape Grim. The highest mountain is Mt Ossa, (1617m) which is in the north west, near Queenstown, on the west coast. South of Queenstown is the beautiful Hartz Mountains National Park.

3 Grammar: Present Perfect

1 Look at the advertisement and underline the English-speaking places Russell has visited.

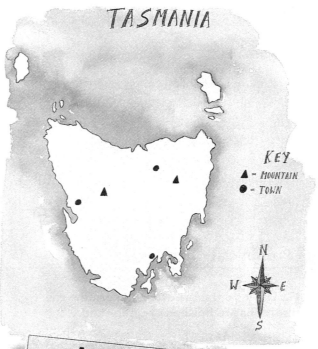

2 Write questions and answers about the places Russell has visited.

1 [Fiji] *Has Russell been to Fiji?*
  Yes, he has.
2 [Singapore] _____
  _____
3 [Tahiti] _____
  _____
4 [Indonesia] _____
  I don't know.
5 [Japan] _____
  _____
6 [The United States] _____
  _____
7 [Thailand] _____
  _____
8 [Beijing] _____
  _____

4 Conversation

Complete the telephone conversation with Russell.

YOU: Is that Russell?
RUSSELL: Yes it is
YOU: *Have you ever been to Tasmania?*
RUSSELL: Yes, _____
YOU: _____?
RUSSELL: It's south of Australia.
YOU: _____?
RUSSELL: Hobart.
YOU: When _____?
RUSSELL: Last year.
YOU: _____?
RUSSELL: It's beautiful. Really lovely.
YOU: _____?
RUSSELL: Yes, lots of very good hotels.
YOU: Are there any national parks?
RUSSELL: _____
YOU: Well, thanks a lot, Russell. You've been very helpful.
RUSSELL: _____
YOU: Bye.

5 Speaking

🔊 **Imagine you are Russell. Listen to the cassette and answer the questions.**

Example:
CASSETTE: Is that Russell
YOU: Yes, it is

6 Reading

Read this book advertisement and answer the questions.

1 What is the writer's name?
2 What is name of the book?
3 Is it fiction or non-fiction?
4 What country is it about?
5 Has he been there before?
6 How long ago?
7 How much does the book cost in England?

7 Listening

🔊 Listen to this interview with the travel writer Rachel Marks. Complete the chart while you listen.

	Country	When visited	Opinion
1		*recently*	
2			
3			
4			

8 Grammar: Present Perfect

Look at these photographs from Rachel Marks' photograph album. Write sentences about her experience.

1 (visit) **She's visited New York.**
2 (be) _____
3 (work) _____
4 (live) _____
5 (write) _____

New York
Signing my book, London
Middle East
Ireland

9 Conversation

Put the sentences in the correct order to make a conversation.

1 What was Hong Kong like? ____
2 Yes, and I've been to Macao, too. ____
3 No, never. ____
4 What are you reading? **1**
5 Have you ever been to Singapore? ____
6 It was fascinating. ____
7 It's a book about Singapore. ____
8 What about Hong Kong? ____

10 Pronunciation: sentence stress

🔊 Listen to the cassette and write the sentences. Then mark the main stress in each sentence.

Example
1 Is it the most interesting place you've been to?

11 Writing

Organise this information and re-write it to make one paragraph of only two sentences.

1 Hobart has a population of 127,000.
2 Tasmania is a state of Australia.
3 The capital of Tasmania is Hobart.
4 Tasmania is south-east of the continent of Australia.
5 Tasmania consists of one large island and several smaller islands.
6 Hobart is in the south.

Tasmania is a state of Australia, consisting of
_____
_____
_____

Unit 18

1 Vocabulary: clothes

Complete the crossword.

Across
1, 5, 6, 7, 8, 9, 11

Down
1, 2, 3, 4, 6, 8, 10

2 Listening

🔊 Listen and tick the sentence you hear.

1. Can you wash the dog, please?
   Can you watch the dog, please?
2. Do you like chips?
   Do you like ships?
3. Can you cash this for me?
   Can you catch this for me?
4. What would you like? You choose.
   What would you like? New shoes.
5. Are those animals cheap?
   Are those animals sheep?
6. Would you like a cherry?
   Would you like a sherry?
7. I'm looking for the shops.
   I'm looking for the chops.

3 Vocabulary: family

1 Match the words with their definitions.

granddaughter   cousin   great-aunt
stepdaughter   niece   sister-in-law

1 the daughter of your uncle or aunt
   cousin

2 the sister of your husband or wife

3 the daughter of your brother or sister

4 the sister of your grandparent

5 the daughter of your husband or wife, by a previous marriage

6 the daughter of your son or daughter.

2 Write the male forms for the words.

1 granddaughter   *grandson*
2 cousin
3 great-aunt
4 stepdaughter
5 niece
6 sister-in-law

Catherine of Aragon was born in 1485, the youngest daughter of Ferdinand and Isabella of Spain. She married Arthur, the elder brother of Henry VIII of England, but when Arthur died (aged 15) she married Henry. They had one daughter, Mary. The marriage was a happy one until Henry fell in love with Anne Boleyn. He tried to divorce Catherine but the Pope refused. This led to the break with Rome.

Catherine of Aragon

Philip II

Philip II of Spain (1527–98) was the son of Charles I of Spain. Charles was the son of Philip I and Juana the Mad, second daughter of Ferdinand and Isabella. Philip II married four times, his second wife being Mary I of England, daughter of Henry VIII and Catherine of Aragon.

Philip I <u>m</u> _____   _____ <u>m</u> _____
                                                    |
_____   _____ <u>m</u> _____   Catherine <u>m</u> (1) _____
                                                          (2) _____
_____ <u>m</u> _____   _____

4 Reading

1 **Read the two texts above and complete the family trees.**

2 **Look at the family trees and decide how Catherine was related to Philip II. Choose the correct answer.**

Catherine was:
a Philip's grandmother
b Philip's great-aunt
c Philip's cousin
d Philip's mother-in-law
e Philip's stepmother

5 Grammar: adverbs

Complete the sentences with an adverb or adjective.

1 She reads slowly. She's a ___*slow*___ reader.
2 He drives _____. He's a careful driver.
3 They're good players. They play _____.
4 He's a fast typist. He types _____.
5 I'm a _____ learner. I learn quickly.
6 He's a polite child. He behaves _____.
7 She writes well. She's a _____ writer.
8 I'm a light sleeper. I sleep very _____.

6 Speaking

🖭 **Listen to the cassette and disagree, using *really*.**

Example:
CASSETTE: This restaurant is quite expensive.
YOU: I think it's really expensive!

7 Listening

📼 Listen to the story and number the pictures in the correct order.

8 Grammar: too/very

Circle the correct word – too, very or both

1 The princess was too/*very*/beautiful.
2 It was too/very cold to be out of doors.
3 It was too/very late to go home.
4 The prince was too/very kind.
5 The bed was too/very high. But she climbed in.
6 The pea was too/very small.

9 Grammar: have to/don't have to

1 Make questions using *have to*. Then try to guess the job.

1 (work hard) *Do you have to work hard?*
 Yes, I do.
2 (travel a lot) _____
 Yes, I do.
3 (use your hands) _____
 No, I don't.
4 (speak in public) _____
 Yes, I do.
5 (work at night) _____
 No, I don't.
6 (wear a crown) _____
 Yes, I do.
7 Are you a _____
 Yes, I am!

2 Write sentences using *don't/doesn't have to*.

1 (Kings and queens/pay taxes)
 Kings and queens don't have to pay taxes.
2 (Queens/take public transport)
 _____
3 (A king/pay rent)
 _____
4 (Kings and queens/have a passport)
 _____
5 (The Queen/cook)
 _____
6 (Princes and princesses/work)
 _____
7 (Kings and queens/drive)
 _____

10 Writing

❍ **What do you like about your work or your school? Write a paragraph about it.**

Try to include these expressions:
I quite like/I really like …
I have to/I don't have to …

Unit 19

1 Vocabulary

Complete the text (in the past), using expressions with *get*.

Victor was born in 1900. He met Dora when he was nineteen: they fell in love and they *got engaged*. Two years later they _____ and lived in a small flat in Dorking. Victor got a job in a furniture factory, but when he was twenty-seven he got hepatitis. He stopped work. He _____ and nearly died. But after a month in hospital he _____ and went home to Dora. But he was too ill to work again and he lost the job at the factory. Dora _____ _____ of nursing Victor. She decided to leave. They _____ and Dora went to Australia. Years passed and Victor _____. He got depressed and lonely. And then one day …

2 Grammar: auxiliary verbs

Complete the sentences with *do/did/will*.

1 *Will* you still love me when I am 64?
2 _____ you like this music?
3 What _____ you wear to the party tomorrow?
4 When _____ you finish school yesterday?
5 I think I _____ retire when I am 60.
6 What time _____ you get home every day?
7 When we are married, we _____ buy a flat.
8 _____ you watch TV last night?
9 How often _____ you watch TV these days?
10 _____ it rain tomorrow?

3 Listening

Listen to the cassette. Decide if the sentences are the *same* or *different*.

1 *same*
2 _____
3 _____
4 _____
5 _____
6 _____
7 _____

4 Puzzle

Can you answer this question?

I will be 20 when my brother is 30. My sister will be 30 when I am 35. My sister will be the same age as my brother is now when I am 25. How old am I now?

_____

5 Speaking

Listen to the cassette, look at the pictures, and answer the questions.

Example:
CASSETTE: So, you're going to stay in a hotel. What will you do when you arrive?
YOU: I'll unpack my case.

6 Vocabulary: houses

Read the note to Ali and complete the crossword.

Dear Ali,
Welcome to our ___*flat*___ [10 across]. You'll find the key when you come up the front _____ [8 down]: it's under the _____ [13 down] in front of the door. The switch for the _____ [1 down] heater is in the kitchen _____ [4 down], above the fridge. The flat is centrally _____ [3 across] so you'll be nice and warm. The outdoor _____ [9 across] is a nice place to eat on a sunny day. Always lock the _____ [6 down] if you go out. If you need to do any ironing, the _____ [11 down] is in the kitchen. It's best if you use the shower because the _____ [5 down] takes a long time to fill. The upstairs _____ [5 across] is prepared for you: I hope you like the bed. If you want to work, there is a desk in my _____ [7 down]. If you want to watch TV or use the _____ [2 down], feel free: we have lots of good films. There are only two _____ [12 across] in the building: the neighbours, who live _____ [14 across], are very friendly. If you need any help, go down and ask them. Enjoy your stay!

7 Listening

🔊 **Listen to the conversation, look at the advertisements below and answer the question.**

Which house do they choose: a, b, c, d or e.

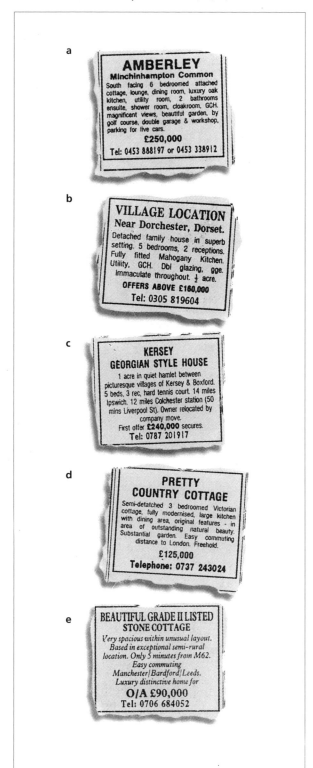

8 Reading

1 Put this description of a flat in the correct order. Number the sentences 1–8.

a Next to the bathroom, on your left when you come in, there's a bedroom. ____

b It's on the second floor. ____

c The bedroom opens on to a small balcony. ____

d When you come in the front door, there is a small hall. ____

e Next to the living room is the kitchen. ____

f My flat is very small. _1_

g Opposite the kitchen there is a bathroom. ____

h The first room on the right of the hall is the living room. ____

2 Draw a plan of the flat.

9 Writing

○ Write a description of your flat or house, and draw a plan.

1 Vocabulary: education

Circle the word that is different in each group.

1 student   pupil   (teacher)   learner
2 school   library   university   college
3 desk   blackboard   map   sofa
4 biology   French   physics   chemistry
5 examination   learn   study   practise

2 Pronunciation: word stress

▣ **Listen to the cassette and mark the stress on these words.**

1 technology
2 chemistry
3 biology
4 examinations
5 geography
6 mathematics
7 arithmetic
8 university
9 library
10 education

3 Speaking

▣ **Listen to the cassette and respond to the questions.**

Example:
CASSETTE: Do you want to read in English?
YOU: Yes, reading in English is really important.

4 Reading

1 Look at this end-of-term school report.

Match the comments with the correct subjects.

Name:	TESSA HAYES	
Year level:	FIVE	
Term:	TWO	

Subject	%	Comment
Reading	75%	Tessa enjoys games and gymnastics.
Writing	90	Works hard but she is not good with numbers.
Oral communication	85	She is a good listener and a good speaker, and she participates in class discussions.
Mathematics	45	Tessa is a member of the school choir and she enjoys painting.
Art/Music/Drama	65	Tessa reads fiction and non-fiction with fluency.
Science	70%	She is an imaginative story-writer. Her spelling and punctuation are good.
Physical Education	50	Tessa is an enthusiastic researcher and has done excellent projects.

2 Read this letter from Tessa. She is now in Level Six. Answer the questions about Tessa's day at school.

1 Does she like mathematics?
No, she doesn't.

2 Does she like language?

3 Is she good at spelling?

4 Is she good at writing?

5 Can you find any spelling mistakes in Tessa's letter? Can you correct them for her? Make a list.
suppose

> I hurried into my classroom. First we had Spelling, thats O.K. I supose. I got eighteen out of twenty words, my usal. Next we had a Maths test Yuck! I really don't like Maths especially tests. Then we got to wright a story about "A Day In The Life Of a Fifty ¢ Coin." "GREAT", I LOVE Story Writting Probley because I'm quite good at it.
> My next lesson was after reccess it was language. My Teache Mrs Sheere write some questions on the board and we have to wright the answers in our books. I like that quite alot, proble my second favourite.
> Anyway after language we can do anything..... play a game, play on the computer.... anything. That's really fun
> Ding a ling, Dingaling! there's the lunch bell.

5 Grammar: review

Correct the sentences.

1 Tessa have ten years.
Tessa is ten.

2 She no like maths.

3 Her grammar is more better than her spelling.

4 Why you no like music?

5 He write English very good.

6 We haven't got no books.

7 What is doing Tessa?

8 She practising his spelling.

6 Listening

🔊 Listen to the teacher describing her daily routine. Complete her timetable.

Time	Subject/Activity
	Teacher gets to work
9.15 – 9.45	
	Maths
11.00 – 12.30	
12.30	
	Games/P.E.
3.45	
	Teacher goes home

7 Writing

Use this information about Tessa to write a paragraph about Tessa's school life. Start like this:

Tessa Hayes is nearly 11. She is in …

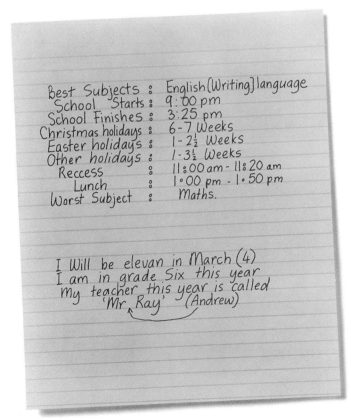

Best Subjects : English (Writing) language
School Starts : 9:00 pm
School Finishes : 3:25 pm
Christmas holidays : 6-7 Weeks
Easter holidays : 1-2½ Weeks
Other holidays : 1-3½ Weeks
Recess : 11:00 am - 11:20 am
Lunch : 1:00 pm - 1:50 pm
Worst Subject : Maths.

I will be eleven in March (4)
I am in grade Six this year
My teacher this year is called
'Mr. Ray' (Andrew)

8 Quiz

Look back at the book and answer these questions.

1 When was Armand Hammer born?

2 When did Shakespeare die?

3 How do you say *thank you* in Japanese?

4 What's the address of the Friendship Hotel, Beijing?

5 When is Diwali celebrated?

6 How many people speak Hungarian?

7 How big is Catalonia?

8 How old was C.P. Cavafy when he died?

9 Where is Thanksgiving celebrated?

10 When did Kodaly write Háry János?

11 What is the highest mountain in South America?

12 How far is Reading from London?

13 Who was the daughter of Catherine of Aragon and Henry VIII?

14 What is the capital of Tasmania?

15 Who wrote *Down Home*?

Vocabulary building

This section is to help you remember vocabulary. After you have completed each unit in the Workbook, turn to this page and add as many words as you can to the list for that unit.

1 Breakfast

coffee   butter
tea   cheese
milk   bread
sugar   toast
egg

_____
_____
_____
_____

2 Places

bank
shops
hotel
restaurant
post office
cinema
school

_____
_____
_____
_____

3 Family

mother
father
parent
children
sister
brother
daughter

_____
_____
_____

4 Interests and activities

sport
music
reading
films
travelling
skiing
cooking
tennis

_____
_____
_____
_____
_____

5 Nationalities

Dutch
Portuguese
Turkish
British
Egyptian
Japanese
Indonesian

_____
_____
_____

6 Jobs

teacher
doctor
actor
waiter
student
politician
dentist

_____
_____
_____

7 Hotel facilities

room
bathroom
swimming pool
car park
hairdresser's
bar

_____
_____
_____
_____

8 Clothes

trousers   jacket
shirt   shoes
jeans   sweater
dress   suit

_____
_____
_____
_____

9 The body

head
back
shoulder
arm
hand
leg
foot (feet)
face
stomach

_____
_____
_____
_____

10 Language

word
sentence
spelling
pronunciation
grammar
verb
plural

_____
_____
_____
_____

11 Characteristics

intelligent
attractive
beautiful
handsome
kind
good-looking
slim

_____
_____
_____
_____

12 Food

meat
chicken
fish
vegetables
tomato
lettuce
onion
yoghurt
oil
sauce
apple

_____
_____
_____

13 Weather

rain
wind
sun
storm
foggy
icy

_____
_____
_____
_____

14 Health

healthy
ill
headache
a cold
stomachache

_____
_____
_____
_____

15 Celebrations

party
marriage
birthday
Christmas
festival
present

_____
_____
_____

16 Size and weight

big
small
heavy
light
tall
long
large

_____
_____
_____

17 Geography

country
city
island
village
north
east

_____
_____
_____
_____

18 Relations

married
divorced
sister-in-law
stepchild
single
wife
engaged

_____
_____
_____

19 Accommodation

house
flat
kitchen
bedroom
balcony
front door
central-heating

_____
_____
_____

20 Education

university
library
mathematics
writing
physics
pupil

_____
_____
_____

Grammar summary

1 Adjectives	8 Prepositions
Position	Place
Comparatives and superlatives	in/at/next to/ between, etc.
Opposites	Time
2 Adverbs	at/in/from/to/on
Regular	Manner
Irregular	by + transport
3 Conjunctions	With certain verbs
and/or	come from
and/but	go to
Why/because	get to
4 Determiners	**9 Question words**
Articles	**10 Verbs**
a/an	Present
the	be
(-)	can
Some and any	have got
+ uncountable nouns	do
+ countable plural nouns	like
This/that/these/those	Other verbs
singular	have to
plural	should
5 Nouns	would like
Regular plurals	Present Continuous
Irregular plurals	wear
6 Possession	Present Perfect
Possessive 's	go
Possessive adjectives	Past
7 Pronouns	be
Subject/object	like
It as an empty subject	Future
	going to
	will
	Imperatives
	-ing form

1 Adjectives

• Position

Adjectives describe nouns and have no plural form. They come before nouns or after the verb *to be*.

A *big* breakfast
3 *black* coffees
She's *American*

• Comparatives and superlatives

Comparatives compare two things or people. Superlatives compare more than two things or people.

Regular

Adjective	Comparative	Superlative
old	older	the oldest
heavy	heavier	the heaviest
expensive	more expensive	the most expensive

Irregular

Adjective	Comparative	Superlative
good	better	the best
bad	worse	the worst

Example: A motorbike is *more expensive than* a bicycle. A car is *the most expensive*.

• Opposites

Opposites with -un

Adjective	Negative adjective
happy	unhappy
intelligent	unintelligent
attractive	unattractive
kind	unkind
friendly	unfriendly
comfortable	uncomfortable

Other opposites

Adjective	Negative adjective
clean	dirty
good	bad
cheap	expensive
fast	slow

2 Adverbs

Adverbs give extra information about verbs and answer the question *How?*
A: How does she work?
B: She works *quickly/carefully/fast/well*, etc.

Regular

Adjective	Adverb
bad	badly
quick	quickly
easy	easily

Irregular

Adjective	Adverb
good	well
fast	fast

3 Conjunctions

Conjunctions connect words and ideas in sentences.

and/or
Tea + coffee = tea *and* coffee
Tea/coffee = tea *or* coffee?

and/but
+ +
I like tea *and* coffee.
+ −
I like tea *but* I don't like coffee.

Why/because
Why does he go to school?   Because he's a teacher.
Why have I got presents?   Because it's your birthday.

4 Determiners

Determiners come before nouns or noun phrases and give them extra meaning.

• Articles

a/an
Used, for example, to describe a place where more than one exists.
Paris is *a* city in France. (There are lots of cities in France).
Zambia is *a* country in Africa. (There are lots of countries in Africa).

66

the
Used, for example, to describe a place where only one exists.
Lusaka is *the* capital of Zambia. (There is only one capital).
***The* is also used with *north*, *south*, *east* and *west*.**
Hiroshima is in *the* south of Japan.

(–)
Used, for example, with continents, countries or towns.
I live in (–) Africa.
I live in (–) Zambia.
I live in (–) Lusaka.

• *Some* and *any* + nouns

	Positive	Negative	Question
Uncountable nouns	some	not any	any
Countable plural nouns	some	not any	any

Uncountable nouns: I've got *some* sugar but I haven't got *any* milk. Have you got *any*?
Countable plural nouns: I've got *some* apples but I haven't got *any* oranges. Have you got *any*?

• *This/that/these/those*

Singular	Plural
This pen is blue.	*These* pens are green.
That pen is black.	*Those* pens are red.

5 Nouns

Nouns are the names of people, animals, places or things.

• Regular

Singular	Plural
a restaurant	2 restaurants
an egg	6 eggs

Nouns ending in *o/s/ss/ch/x*

Singular	Plural
a sandwich	2 sandwiches
a potato	2 potatoes

Nouns ending in y

Singular	Plural
baby	babies
family	families

• Irregular

Singular	Plural
person	people
man	men
child	children
woman	women

6 Possession

Possession expresses who things belong to.

• Possessive *'s*

Questions	Answers
Whose pen is this?	It's *Susan's*.
Whose parents are they?	They're *George's*.

With two or more names, write *'s* with the last name only.
Whose child is she? She's Alison and *Martin's*.

• Possessive adjectives

Subject pronoun	Possessive adjective
I	my
you	your
she	her
he	his
it	its
we	our
you	your
they	their

Example: Maria is with *her* father.

7 Pronouns

Pronouns are words used in place of nouns.

• Subject/object

Subject pronoun	Object pronoun
I	me
you	you
she	her
he	him
it	it
we	us
you	you
they	them

Example: She likes *him* because he's kind.

• *It* for weather, time and distances

***It* is used as an empty subject (with no real meaning).**
It is foggy and it is raining.
It is winter/spring/summer/autumn.
It is three o'clock.
It is Tuesday.
How long does *it* take?
It is 250 metres to the bank.

8 Prepositions

Prepositions are used to express a relationship between one person or thing and another.

• Place

in/at

In	At
in Australia	*at* home
in London	*at* work
in a hotel	*at* school

next to, between, in front of, behind, on the left/right of

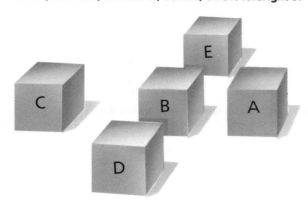

A is *next to* B
B is *between* A and C
D is *in front of* B
E is *behind* B
C is *on the left of* B
A is *on the right of* B

next to, near, far from, a long way from, opposite

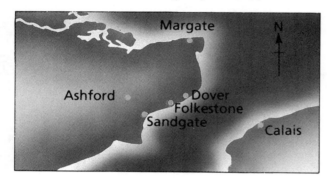

Folkestone is the town next to Dover. It is near Sandgate. It isn't far from Ashford but it's a long way from Margate. Folkestone is opposite Calais in France.

• Time

at/in/from/to/on

What time do you have breakfast?
At 7 o'clock *in* the morning.

What time are the shops open?
From 9 am *to* 5.30 pm, *from* Monday *to* Saturday.

I go on holiday *in* July.
I went to Belgium *in* 1977.
I start work *on* Monday.
It's my birthday *on* 2nd October.

• Manner

by + transport

I go to work
   by bus
   by taxi
   by car
   by train
or I walk

• With certain verbs

come from	I *come from* Switzerland.
go to	I *go to* work at 7 am.
get to	I *get to* the office at 7.30 am.

9 Question words

Question	Answer
What is this?	A photograph.
Who is this man?	Mr Smith.
Whose father is he?	Thomas and Kate's.
When was he born?	1952.
Where does he work?	In an office.
Which office does he work in?	The school office.
Why does he like his job?	Because it's very interesting.
How much does he earn?	£25,000 a year.
How many children has he got?	Two.
How old are they?	Six and eleven years old.

10 Verbs

• Present: Key verbs: *be/can/have got/do/like*

> The Present form can be used to
> - give personal details
> - talk about habits and routines
> - talk about present states
> - talk about likes and dislikes

be (+ nouns and adjectives)
Positive and negative

I	am		
You/we/they	are	(not)	late.
She/he/it	is		

Question

Am	I	
Are	you/we/they	late?
Is	she/he/it	

can and *can't* (ability + possibility)
Positive and negative

I You/we/they She/he/it	can	(not)	swim. go.

Question

Can	I you/we/they she/he/it	swim? go?

have (got) (possession, families and illnesses)
Positive and negative

I/you/we/they	have	(not)	got a big family.
She/he/it	has		

Question

Have	I/you/we/they	got a big family?
Has	she/he/it	

do
Positive

I/you/we/they	do	exercises regularly.
she/he/it	does	

Negative

I/you/we/they	do	not do exercises regularly.
She/he/it	does	

Question

Do	I/you/we/they	do exercises regularly?
Does	she/he/it	

like (regular Present Simple form)
Positive

I/you/we/they	like	tea. dancing.
She/he/it	likes	

Negative

I/you/we/they	don't	like	tea. dancing.
She/he/it	doesn't		

Question

Do	I/you/we/they	like	tea? dancing?
Does	she/he/it		

• Other verbs: *have to/should/would like*

have to (obligation)
Positive

I/you/we/they	have to	go.
She/he/it	has to	

Negative

I/you/we/they	don't	have to go.
She/he/it	doesn't	

Question

Do	I/you/we/they	have to go?
Does	she/he/it	

should (advice)
Positive

I/you/we/they	should	phone.
She/he/it		come.

Negative

I/you/we/they	shouldn't	phone.
She/he/it		come.

Question

Should	I/you/we/they	phone?
	she/he/it	come?

would like (offers and requests)

Offer
A: Would you like a drink?
B: Yes, please.

Request
A: I'd like a Coke.
B: Here you are.

• Present Continuous

> The Present Continuous form can be used to express an activity in progress now.

Positive and negative

I	am		wearing a jacket
You/we/they	are	(not)	
She/he/it	is		

Question

Am	I	wearing a jacket?
Are	you/we/they	
Is	she/he/it	

• Present Perfect (experience)

> The Present Perfect can be used to talk about experience.

go
Positive and negative

I/you/we/they	have	(not)	been to Spain.
She/he/it	has		

Question

Have	I/you/we/they	been to Spain?
Has	she/he/it	

- **Past**

  The Past form can be used to express
  - historical events
  - biographical events
  - actions which happened at a specific time in the past and are now finished.

  be
  Positive and negative

I/she/he/it	was	(not)	late.
You/we/they	were		born in Madrid.

  Question

Was	I/she/he/it	late?
Were	you/we/they	born in Madrid?

  like **(regular Past Simple form)**
  Positive

I/you/we/they	liked her.
She/he/it	

  Negative

I/you/we/they	did not (didn't)	like her.
She/he/it		

  Question

Did	I/you/we/they	like her?
	she/he/it	

- **Future**

  going to **(future plans)**

  Going to can be used to express
  - future plans
  - decisions made before the time of speaking.

  Positive and negative

I	am		
You/we/they	are	(not)	going to watch TV tonight.
She/he/it	is		

  Question

Am	I	
Are	you/we/they	going to watch TV tonight?
Is	she/he/it	

Will **(future predictions)**

Will can be used to express
- future predictions
- offers and decisions made at the time of speaking.

Positive

I/you/we/they	will	visit the USA.
She/he/it		

Negative

I/you/we/they	will not	visit the USA.
She/he/it	won't	

Question

Will	I/you/we/they	visit the USA?
	she/he/it	

- **Imperatives**

  Imperatives are used, for example, to give instructions and street directions.

Positive	**Negative**
Stop!	Don't stop!
Pull!	Don't pull!

- *-ing* **form**

  The *-ing* form can be used
  - for activities and interests
  - after the verb *like*.

  Activities
  Read*ing* is one of my interests.

  Like **+ verb +** ***ing***
  I like read*ing*.

Irregular verbs

Infinitive	Past Simple	Past participle
be /biː/	**was** /wəz, wɒz/	**been** /bɪn, biːn/
become /bɪˈkʌm/	**became** /bɪˈkeɪm/	**become** /bɪˈkʌm/
bring /brɪŋ/	**brought** /brɔːt/	**brought** /brɔːt/
buy /baɪ/	**bought** /bɔːt/	**bought** /bɔːt/
can /kən, kæn/	**could** /kʊd/	**been able** /bɪn ˈeɪbl/
catch /kætʃ/	**caught** /kɔːt/	**caught** /kɔːt/
choose /tʃuːz/	**chose** /tʃəʊz/	**chosen** /ˈtʃəʊzn/
come /kʌm/	**came** /keɪm/	**come** /kʌm/
cost /kɒst/	**cost** /kɒst/	**cost** /kɒst/
dig /dɪg/	**dug** /dʌg/	**dug** /dʌg/
do /dʊ, də, duː/	**did** /dɪd/	**done** /dʌn/
draw /drɔː/	**drew** /druː/	**drawn** /drɔːn/
drink /drɪŋk/	**drank** /dræŋk/	**drunk** /drʌŋk/
drive /draɪv/	**drove** /drəʊv/	**driven** /ˈdrɪvn/
eat /iːt/	**ate** /et/	**eaten** /ˈiːtn/
feed /fiːd/	**fed** /fed/	**fed** /fed/
find /faɪnd/	**found** /faʊnd/	**found** /faʊnd/
fly /flaɪ/	**flew** /fluː/	**flown** /fləʊn/
get /get/	**got** /gɒt/	**got** /gɒt/
give /gɪv/	**gave** /geɪv/	**given** /ˈgɪvn/
go /gəʊ/	**went** /went/	**gone** /gɒn/ **been** /bɪn, biːn/
have /həv, hæv/	**had** /(h)əd, hæd/	**had** /hæd/
know /nəʊ/	**knew** /njuː/	**known** /nəʊn/
lose /luːz/	**lost** /lɒst/	**lost** /lɒst/
learn /lɜːn/	**learnt** /lɜːnt/	**learnt** /lɜːnt/
leave /liːv/	**left** /left/	**left** /left/
make /meɪk/	**made** /meɪd/	**made** /meɪd/
meet /miːt/	**met** /met/	**met** /met/
pay /peɪ/	**paid** /peɪd/	**paid** /peɪd/
put /pʊt/	**put** /pʊt/	**put** /pʊt/
read /riːd/	**read** /red/	**read** /red/
ride /raɪd/	**rode** /rəʊd/	**ridden** /ˈrɪdn/
run /rʌn/	**ran** /ræn/	**run** /rʌn/
say /seɪ/	**said** /sed/	**said** /sed/
see /siː/	**saw** /sɔː/	**seen** /siːn/
sell /sel/	**sold** /səʊld/	**sold** /səʊld/
send /send/	**sent** /sent/	**sent** /sent/
show /ʃəʊ/	**showed** /ʃəʊd/	**shown** /ʃəʊn/
sing /sɪŋ/	**sang** /sæŋ/	**sung** /sʌŋ/
sit /sɪt/	**sat** /sæt/	**sat** /sæt/
sleep /sliːp/	**slept** /slept/	**slept** /slept/
speak /spiːk/	**spoke** /spəʊk/	**spoken** /ˈspəʊkn/
spend /spend/	**spent** /spent/	**spent** /spent/
stand /stænd/	**stood** /stʊd/	**stood** /stʊd/
swim /swɪm/	**swam** /swæm/	**swum** /swʌm/
take /teɪk/	**took** /tʊk/	**taken** /ˈteɪkn/
teach /tiːtʃ/	**taught** /tɔːt/	**taught** /tɔːt/
tell /tel/	**told** /təʊld/	**told** /təʊld/
think /θɪŋk/	**thought** /θɔːt/	**thought** /θɔːt/
understand /ʌndəˈstænd/	**understood** /ʌndəˈstʊd/	**understood** /ʌndəˈstʊd/
wear /weəʳ/	**wore** /wɔːʳ/	**worn** /wɔːn/
win /wɪn/	**won** /wʌn/	**won** /wʌn/
write /raɪt/	**wrote** /rəʊt/	**written** /ˈrɪtn/

Tapescript

Unit 0

Exercise 3
1 V–I–D–E–O
2 B–A–N–K
3 H–O–T–E–L
4 T–E–N–N–I–S
5 F–O–O–T–B–A–L–L
6 R–E–S–T–A–U–R–A–N–T
7 H–O–S–P–I–T–A–L
8 P–I–Z–Z–A
9 C–I–G–A–R–E–T–T–E

Exercise 4
video   tennis   hospital
bank   football   pizza
hotel   restaurant cigarette

Unit 1

Exercise 5
A: Good morning.
B: Good morning. I'd like to order breakfast, please.
A: Certainly. What's your room number?
B: Room three–oh–one.
A: Four–oh–one.
B: *Three*–oh–one.
A: For how many?
B: For two.
A: Breakfast for two. Tea or coffee?
B: Pardon?
A: Would you prefer tea or coffee?
B: Two black coffees, please.
A: Anything else?
B: Yes, one toast and marmalade, and one egg and bacon.
A: One toast and marmalade, and one egg and bacon. Anything else?
B: No, that's all thank you.
A: Thank you.

Exercise 6
1 Good morning.
2 I'd like to order breakfast, please.
3 Two black coffees, please.
4 One toast and marmalade.
5 One egg and bacon.
6 One toast and marmalade and one egg and bacon.
7 That's all, thank you.

Exercise 8
a 0223
b 315 697
c 017 569 215
d 39 01 56
e 318 01 22
f 018 543 909
g 010 39
h 010 349 456 209
i 010 648 98 971
j 999

Unit 2

Exercise 4
In Ireland shops are open from nine to six, and banks are open from 9.30 am to 12.30, Monday to Friday and they open again from 1.30 to 3.00. Shops are open on Saturdays but banks are closed on Saturdays and Sundays. Cinemas are open from 2.30 to 10.30, and pubs are open from 11.00 am to 12.00 pm every day except Sunday when they close at 11.00.

Exercise 6
1 bottle of milk
  Can I have a bottle of milk, please?
2 map
  Can I have a map, please?
3 beer
  Can I have a beer, please?
4 orange juice
  Can I have an orange juice, please?
5 packet of cigarettes
  Can I have a packet of cigarettes, please?
6 list of hotels
  Can I have a list of hotels, please?
7 list of hotels and restaurants
  Can I have a list of hotels and restaurants, please?

Exercise 9
My name is Seamus and I come from Ireland. I work in an office in the centre of Dublin. Every day I have breakfast at about 7.30 in the morning and I go to the office at eight. I get to the office at about 8.30, depending on the traffic. I work in the office all morning, and have lunch in a café at about one. I go home at about six. In the evening, on Tuesday and Thursday, I go to a Spanish class. I get to the class at 7.30. I get back home at about nine or 9.30.

Unit 3

Exercise 6
Hello, my name is Jan. I come from Columbus, Ohio. My father's name is Gary and my mother is called Doreen. (D–O–R–E–E–N.) My parents are separated and I live with my mother. I've got two brothers and a sister. My brothers' names are Nat and Jeff (J–E–F–F), and my sister is called Linda. Nat is married: his wife's name is Catherine. They haven't got any children yet. Well, that's my family.

Exercise 10
1 Are you married?
2 Is she English?
3 Are they sisters?
4 Have you got any children?
5 Have you got any brothers?
6 Have you got any sisters?
7 Have you got any brothers or sisters?
8 Are your brothers and sisters married?

Unit 4

Exercise 4

1 I like cooking. What about you?
  I like cooking too.
2 I like travelling. What about you?
  I like travelling too.
3 I like reading magazines. What about you?
  I like reading magazines too.
4 I like films. What about you?
  I like films too.
5 I like writing letters. What about you?
  I like writing letters too.
6 I like watching television. What about you?
  I like watching television too.
7 I like listening to the radio. What about you?
  I like listening to the radio too.

Exercise 7

My name's Hilda. I live in Utrecht which is a large city in Holland. I live with my sister Carolien. We both study economics at the University of Utrecht. This is my daily routine: I get up at about eight and go to the University with Carolien. I have breakfast at the University. I study all morning and have lunch at two. At three I study in the library. I get home at about four. Carolien usually does the housework but I cook dinner. After dinner I read or listen to music. I normally go to bed at about one.

Exercise 9

GÜL: My name's Gül. I like coffee and tea but I don't like wine or beer.

ROSA: I'm Rosa. I like wine – red wine, and coffee – black coffee. But I don't like tea or beer.

ANDRÉ: My name's André and I'm from Belgium. I like beer very much – Belgian beer, of course. I like tea and coffee, too. Wine? No, I don't like wine that much.

LEILA I'm Leila. My favourite drink is tea – I drink ten cups of tea a day. I don't like coffee very much, nor wine. And beer: Ugh!

Unit 5

Exercise 2

1 Sorry.
2 Sorry!
3 Thank you!
4 Thank you.
5 Please.
6 Please!
7 Excuse me?
8 Excuse me.
9 Excuse me!

Exercise 3

1 How old is Karl?
  I think he's thirteen.
2 How many students are there?
  Thirty.
3 Good morning.
  Can I have fifteen stamps, please?
4 How old are you?
  I'm seventeen. And you?
  I'm nineteen.
5 How much is that, please?
  Fifty pounds.
6 What time do you get home?
  Normally at six fifteen.
7 What's your phone number?
  Have you got a pen?
  Yes.
  It's nine oh five, three four, eight six.
8 Excuse me, have you got the correct time?
  Yes, it's nine forty-five.
  Thank you.
9 Can I have fourteen teas, twelve black coffees, and five white coffees, please.
  Forty teas?
  No, fourteen.

Exercise 7: 2

tea	they	three	to	bye
know	we	do	no	
I	two	bye	say	
hey!	hi!	me	she	

Unit 6

Exercise 1: 3

Yesterday I got up early and washed my hair. I cooked breakfast – eggs and bacon – and listened to the news on the radio. It was a lovely day so I walked to the clinic. I'm a dentist, you see. I worked all morning and afternoon. I got home about six and I watched television for a bit, had dinner, and then, um, I don't remember, um, oh yes, I went to a disco and danced till three in the morning!

Exercise 3

He was born in England in April 1564. He went to work in London. He was an actor and writer. His wife's name was Anne. He wrote 38 plays. He died in 1616.

Exercise 6

1 What's the date? It's the fourth of January.
2 What's the date? It's the twelfth of May.
3 What's the date? It's the twenty-first of August.
4 What's the date? It's the sixteenth of December.
5 What's the date? It's the second of March.
6 What's the date? It's the fifth of July.
7 What's the date? It's the twenty-third of April.
8 What's the date? It's the thirtieth of November.

Unit 7

Exercise 5

1
FRIEND: Did you have a good holiday then, Wim?
WIM: Yes, fantastic. I went to Venice.
FRIEND: Where did you stay?
WIM: In the Excelsior.

2 Hello, my name's Greta. I went to Madrid last July and stayed in the Ritz. It was lovely. I really enjoyed myself. I went to the…

3 Hello, is that the Grand Hotel, Cairo?
...
I said, is that the Grand?
...
I'd like to book a room, please.
...
August. I arrive in Cairo on August the fourth.
...
Brita Ekberg. E–K–B–E–R–G.
...
Brita. B–R–I–T–A.
...
Thank you. Goodbye.

Exercise 8

1 A: What would you like to drink?
   B: I'd like a coffee, please.
2 A: Where are the children?
   B: They're in the swimming pool.
3 A: What's his name?
   B: Barry, I think – or is it Bruce?
4 A: Where do you stay in Istanbul?
   B: Oh, we like the Pera Palace Hotel, actually.
5 A: How much is this perfume?
   B: This one? Twenty Canadian dollars.
6 A: Do you like whisky?
   B: No, I never drink the stuff.
7 A: What does your husband do?
   B: He's a customs officer.
   C: Oh, really?
8 When I'm in Istanbul, I like visiting the market and the mosques.
9 A: How was your hotel?
   B: It was OK. No TV in the room, though.
10 A: Have you got any cigarettes?
    B: No, only these cigars.
11 A: Did you take the children?
    B: No, this was our holiday.

Exercise 11

1 Would you like a double bed or a single bed?
  I'd like a double bed, please.
2 Would you like tea or coffee?
  I'd like tea, please.
3 Would you like a colour TV or a black and white TV?
  I'd like a colour TV, please.
4 Would you like a first class hotel or a second class hotel?
  I'd like a first class hotel, please.
5 Would you like a double room or a single room?
  I'd like a double room, please.

Unit 8

Exercise 3

1 Mark's party is on Saturday.
2 Her father's car is black.
3 Charles started work in March.
4 My aunt can't dance.
5 Martha and Mary aren't from France.
6 There's a bar in the car park.
7 Can I have your landing card?

Exercise 5

A: What's the date?
B: Tuesday. Why?
A: Tuesday the what?
B: The second.
A: Oh no, it's Sheila's birthday tomorrow.
B: It is too.
A: What are we going to get her?
B: Flowers?
A: We can't give her flowers. It's her birthday, not her funeral.
B: Chocolates?
A: She doesn't like chocolates.
B: A compact disc? She likes music.
A: She hasn't got a compact disc player.
B: A book?
A: What book?
B: I don't know. Something about China. She's going to China for her holidays.
A: Hmm. Or a cassette? She's got a cassette player.
B: A cassette of Chinese music.
A: No, I think you're right. A book about China – nice photos and things.
B: Or a Chinese cook book. She loves cooking.
A: That's a good idea. Who's going to buy it?
B: Well, I'm going into town this afternoon. I could ...

Exercise 9

1 have lunch
  Would you like to have lunch with me?
2 have dinner
  Would you like to have dinner with me?
3 come to the cinema
  Would you like to come to the cinema with me?
4 come to the football
  Would you like to come to the football with me?
5 go shopping
  Would you like to go shopping with me?
6 go to Athens
  Would you like to go to Athens with me?
7 come home
  Would you like to come home with me?
8 practise English
  Would you like to practise English with me?

Unit 9

Exercise 2

ASSISTANT: Good morning. Can I help you?
ASSISTANT: Prints or slides?
ASSISTANT: Black and white or colour?
ASSISTANT: How many? 12, 24, or 36?
ASSISTANT: That will be £4.75, please.

Exercise 6

FRIEND: This is a nice one. Where's this?
ANNIE: Oh that – that's last summer in Sicily.
FRIEND: Is that you Annie? In the middle at the back?
ANNIE: Yeah, that's me.
FRIEND: You're so brown. Who's that next to you, on your left? Is that your dad?
ANNIE: No, that's my uncle Jack.
FRIEND: And on your right?
ANNIE: That's Jack's wife, Vera. My aunt Vera.
FRIEND: I like her shorts
ANNIE: And that's Eddie, my brother, in the front, between my father and Sylvia.

FRIEND: Who's Sylvia?
ANNIE: Oh, Sylvia's an Italian woman who was staying in…

Exercise 9

1 No, sorry, I can't come on Saturday.
2 I can come on Friday.
3 Can you move your arm?
4 No, I can't.
5 Who can play tennis here?
6 I can't.
7 I can.
8 Can you come to the party?
9 Bella can't come to dinner.

Unit 10

Exercise 2

1 When's your birthday?
2 The fifteenth of July.
3 The fifteenth of July.
4 Would you like a hamburger?
5 I'd like an ice-cream.
6 Have you got any perfume?
7 Would you like a magazine?
8 Do you speak Chinese?
9 Where's the receptionist?

Exercise 6

BOB: Hello, Anna. Come in. How are you?
ANNA: I'm well. Here's a bottle of wine.
BOB: Thanks. Do you know Claude? Claude, this is Anna.
CLAUDE: Hello Anna.
ANNA: Hi. Are you French?
CLAUDE: No, I'm Canadian. And you?
ANNA: I'm Australian.
BOB: Hello, Martin. Anna, this is a friend of mine from work, Martin.
ANNA: Hello, Martin. I think we met that time…
MARTIN: Anna! Yes, how *are* you?
ANNA: I'm very well, thanks. Martin, this is Claude. Claude is from Canada. Martin works with Bob.
CLAUDE: Oh, really?
ANNA: Where is your girlfriend, Martin?
MARTIN: Who? Gianella? Erm, she's in Italy for a week, on business.
BOB: Claude, what would you like to drink?
CLAUDE: Have you got orange juice?
BOB: I think so. Anna? Martin?
MARTIN: Beer, please, Bob.
ANNA: Nothing for me. What about some music? Who likes rock 'n roll?
MARTIN: Oh, Anna, *not* rock 'n roll.
ANNA: Oh, Martin, don't you like rock 'n roll?
MARTIN: Not very much, no.
BOB: Who can that be?
GIANELLA: Hi!
EVERYONE: *Gianella!*
MARTIN: Hello, Gianella. When did you get back?
BOB: Orange juice, anyone? Beer? Martin? Gianella?

Exercise 7

1 Have you got any orange juice?
  I think so.
2 Martin works with Bob.
  Oh really?
3 I'm from Canada.
  Oh really?
4 Is Anna Australian?
  I think so.
5 Does Martin work with Bob?
  I think so.
6 Gianella's in Italy.
  Oh really?
7 Does Anna like rock 'n roll?
  I think so.
8 Have you got any beer?
  I think so.
9 Martin doesn't like rock 'n roll.
  Oh really?
10 Is Bob married?
   I think so.
11 Bob is married.
   Oh really?

Unit 11

Exercise 3

1
A: So, what's he like then?
B: Who?
A: Your boyfriend, of course.
B: Well, he's got brown eyes…
A: Yes?
B: And he's, well, medium height, well, a bit short actually, I suppose you could say.
A: Mm. What colour's his hair?
B: Oh, he's got dark hair, you know, dark brown. And curly.
A: Hmm. Sounds nice.
B: Oh, yes, he's very good looking. Everyone says so.

2 My favourite teacher at school was my geography teacher, Mrs Andrews. She was quite different from all the other teachers in that she never talked down to you: she was always perfectly natural, a very sincere person, and honest: she told you exactly what she thought, but it was never, you know, malicious or … She was kind, too. I remember once when I missed two weeks' school when I had mumps or measles or something, she made a little summary of all the lessons I had missed, and so when I came back, I didn't have to …

3
A: Personally, I prefer your more traditional sort of dog, you know, a German Shepherd, or a Labrador – an outdoor dog.
B: Do you? They're not very affectionate, though, are they – Alsatians, I mean? I prefer something smaller, like a Terrier, or a Spaniel. I think Spaniels are beautiful.
A: Oh no, Spaniels maybe, but Terriers, no. They bark all the time. I mean, compared to a Labrador, they're actually not very intelligent, Terriers. Not very attractive either. If you have to have a small dog, I suppose a Spaniel …

Exercise 7

1 Patty is married to George.
2 Is Patty married?
3 Yes, she is.
4 Alan and Patty are single.
5 No, they aren't.

75

6 Yes, they are.
7 Gary is on holiday.
8 Has Rita got a daughter?
9 Yes she has.

Exercise 10

1 Was Cleopatra Italian?
   No, she wasn't. She was Egyptian.
2 Was Mozart German?
   No, he wasn't. He was Austrian.
3 Were the Marx Brothers English?
   No, they weren't. They were American.
4 Was Napoleon tall?
   No, he wasn't. He was short.
5 Was Cervantes a politician?
   No, he wasn't. He was a writer.
6 Was Picasso French?
   No, he wasn't. He was Spanish.
7 Were the Andrews Sisters dancers?
   No, they weren't. They were singers.
8 Was Indira Gandhi single?
   No, she wasn't. She was married.

Unit 12

Exercise 3

A: What are you going to make?
B: I was thinking of trying this Turkish dish: Imam Bayıldı.
A: What's that exactly?
B: Stuffed aubergines.
A: Hmm. What do you need for that?
B: Well, aubergines, to start with. Have we got any?
A: No. I'll make a list. Aubergines.
B: Have we got any sugar?
A: Yes. I think so, yes.
B: Oil?
A: What sort?
B: Olive oil.
A: No.
B: How are we off for salt?
A: We've got salt.
B: Have we got any onions?
A: No, we haven't.
B: Tomatoes?
A: We've got a can of tomato purée.
B: No, we need fresh tomatoes.
A: We haven't got any.
B: Have we got any lemons?
A: No.
B: Have we got any garlic?
A: I think we've got some. Yes. We have garlic.
B: Have we got any parsley?
A: No.
B: That's about it. So, who's doing the shopping …

Exercise 7

1 We need some sugar.
2 Have we got any cheese?
3 No, we haven't got any.
4 Yes, we have.
5 We need some onions.
6 Do we need any parsley?
7 Yes, we do.

Exercise 8

1 Was the hotel clean?
   No, it was dirty.
2 Were the taxis cheap?
   No, they were expensive.
3 Were the beaches dirty?
   No, they were clean.
4 Was the food tasty?
   No, it was tasteless.
5 Was the weather hot?
   No, it was cold.
6 Were the restaurants expensive?
   No, they were cheap.
7 Was the train fast?
   No, it was slow.
8 Were the people nice?
   No, they were unfriendly.

Unit 13

Exercise 2

… and here is the weather forecast for tomorrow. Cold weather continues to grip the east coast with strong winds on the Newfoundland coast and snow falling in central Québec. Temperatures will reach minus 7 degrees overnight. Ontario will experience cold foggy weather in the morning. Further west, in Manitoba and Saskatchewan there will be cloud, with some rain in the Lake Winnipeg area. In the far west the weather in British Columbia is warm with sunny conditions, although there will be some morning fog in and around Vancouver. Expected temperatures for tomorrow …

Exercise 7

1 The sun is shining
2 The birds are singing
3 I'm sitting in the garden
4 The children are playing
5 Philip is reading a book
6 A woman is walking into the bank
7 She's wearing a green dress
8 She's wearing a grey jacket
9 She's carrying an umbrella
10 She's leaving the bank

Exercise 8

A: Hello
B: Hello! What's that noise? It sounds like a party. Are you two having a party?
A: No, we're not having a party exactly.
B: Well, are you watching television, then?
A: No, we're not watching television exactly.
B: Oh, you're watching a video, is that it?
A: No, we're not watching a video exactly.
B: Well, are you listening to the radio?
A: No, we're not listening to the radio exactly.
B: Well, you're listening to something. Are you listening to a compact disc?
A: No, we're not listening to a compact disc exactly.
B: Oh, I know. You're playing a computer game. Is that it – are you playing a computer game?
A: No, we're not playing a computer game exactly.
B: I've got it! You're listening to a cassette and practising your English!

Unit 14

Exercise 5

1. What do you do?
2. What do you do?
3. Where do you live?
4. Where do you live?
5. What would you like?
6. What would you like?
7. Are you married?
8. Are you married?
9. What's your flat like?
10. What's your flat like?

Exercise 6

1. What do you do?
   I'm a doctor. What do you do?
2. Where do you live?
   I live in Brighton. Where do you live?
3. Where do you work?
   I work in Bristol. Where do you work?
4. What are you studying?
   I'm studying French. What are you studying?
5. Are you married?
   Yes, I am. Are you married?
6. Have you got any children?
   No, I haven't. Have you got any children?
7. Is your husband English?
   Yes, he is. Is your husband English?
8. What would you like to drink?
   I'd like red wine. What would you like?

Exercise 11

DOCTOR: Well, what seems to be the problem?
PATIENT: I have this ache, doctor.
DOCTOR: Where exactly?
PATIENT: Here, in my stomach.
DOCTOR: That's not your stomach, that's your liver. Let's have a look. Does that hurt?
PATIENT: Ooh!
DOCTOR: Hmm. Do you have any other symptoms?
PATIENT: Well, I have this headache all the time.
DOCTOR: Anything else?
PATIENT: Yes, my back. I get a backache when I work. And I get very tired. I feel tired all the time.
DOCTOR: Let's listen to your heart … Your heart's OK. Breathe deep now. Your lungs are OK. I think it's your liver, I'm afraid, I'm going to have do some tests …

Unit 15

Exercise 3

1. Thank you
2. Thank you!
3. Thank you.
4. Hello.
5. Hello.
6. Happy New Year!
7. Happy New Year.
8. Congratulations.
9. Congratulations.

Exercise 6

A: … and do they celebrate religious festivals there?
B: Well, I don't know. I think since the revolution, no. But I was there for a big political festival.
A: Oh? What was that?
B: Er, it was the 26th July – it's the anniversary of the revolution. It's a national holiday.
A: Oh, what happens?
B: Well, the main thing is the President's speech. That's early in the evening. I was in Havana, but he was speaking in some town somewhere, in the provinces. So I didn't see him. But everyone listens on the radio, or watches on television.
A: How long does that last?
B: Oh, that goes on for quite a while – two or three hours. But first, before that, in the morning, there's a parade and speeches by the local leader of the Communist Party in the town square. Everyone dresses up in their best clothes, the schools and offices close, everyone goes into town, the speeches start and that's how things get going.
A: I see. And later on?
B: Well, after Castro's speech, the music starts and everyone starts drinking beer – which is not rationed on this one day of the year – you can buy as much as you like.
A: It sounds like fun.
B: Yeah, and then everyone goes home for a large dinner – congrí rice, which is a typical Cuban dish made of rice and beans and pork crisps – mm, absolutely delicious.
A: And then?
B: Well, then it's one long party all night!

Unit 16

Exercise 3

INTERVIEWER: Justine, you went to South America didn't you?
JUSTINE: Yes, I did. It was fantastic.
INTERVIEWER: When was that?
JUSTINE: Well, I went there two years ago and travelled around for about two months. First of all I went to Rio and stayed there for about a week, but I did find that expensive – I think the most expensive place that I went, especially the restaurants, and full of tourists too. So, we moved on, we went to, by bus, to Asunción in Paraguay and stayed there for a few days.
INTERVIEWER: What was that like?
JUSTINE: Well, it was very hot actually, I found it too hot so we moved on again. We went north into Brazil and stayed in a town called Corumba.
INTERVIEWER: Right.
JUSTINE: That's on the edge of a wildlife reserve and it's huge. It's the same size as Belgium.
INTERVIEWER: Huh.
JUSTINE: Um, we stayed there a few days. We saw the animals, that was great. Then, from there we had to take a train into Bolivia but that was awful, that was definitely the worst thing that happened to me.
INTERVIEWER: Why?
JUSTINE: Well, we had to spend 24 hours on the train, there were no lights, there were only wooden seats and some people had to stand up for 24 hours, dreadful.
INTERVIEWER: Not something you'd do every day really.
JUSTINE: No, not really. Um, that took us into Bolivia and we stayed in La Paz for a few days and from there we went on to Peru. In Peru actually we visited Machupicchu, which was the most interesting thing for me.
INTERVIEWER: What kind of place is that?
JUSTINE: Well, it's an ancient city and it's actually on the top of a mountain. In fact you can take the train there but you can also walk and it takes three

days to walk over the mountains so we did that, it was great.
INTERVIEWER: Sounds pretty good.
JUSTINE: From there, well that was the end of the holiday I'm afraid, so we went to Lima and I flew home from there.

Exercise 6

1 Take the first street on the left
2 Take the first street on the left, and it's opposite the park
3 Go along this street, and turn left at the traffic lights
4 Go along this street, and turn left at the traffic lights
5 Go along this street, and turn left at the traffic lights, and take the first street on your right, there's a video shop on the corner
6 Go along this street, and turn left at the traffic lights, and take the first street on your right, there's a video shop on the corner

Exercise 7

1 I think this one is the nicest.
   I agree, but this one is nice, too.
2 I think this one is the oldest.
   I agree, but this one is old, too.
3 I think this one is the cheapest.
   I agree, but this one is cheap, too.
4 I think this one is the most interesting.
   I agree, but this one is interesting, too.
5 I think this one is the best.
   I agree, but this one is good, too.
6 I think this one is the most expensive.
   I agree, but this one is expensive, too.
7 I think this one is the worst.
   I agree, but this one is bad, too.

Unit 17

Exercise 5

Is that Russell?
Russell, have you ever been to Tasmania?
Where is it exactly?
What's the capital?
When did you go there?
What's it like?
Are there any good hotels there?
Are there any national parks?
Well, thanks a lot, Russell. You've been very helpful.

Exercise 7

INTERVIEWER: Ms Marks, can I ask you a few questions about your extremely colourful life? Firstly, your most recent book, about China, is your tenth, isn't that so?
RACHEL MARKS: My tenth travel book, yes. I've also written a novel, a book of poems, and a cookbook.
INTERVIEWER: Why China?
RACHEL MARKS: I've been to China a number of times, but I've never written a book about it. I find it fascinating.
INTERVIEWER: Is it the most interesting place you've been to?
RACHEL MARKS: Most interesting, no. The most interesting place I've been to is … let me think … Antarctica.
INTERVIEWER: You've been to the Antarctic?
RACHEL MARKS: Only once. In 1987. It was … it was …
INTERVIEWER: Cold?
RACHEL MARKS: Extremely cold.
INTERVIEWER: You've also been in some very dangerous places. In your book, *Itchy Feet*, you describe a meeting with a tiger.
RACHEL MARKS: Yes, that was in Burma, in '66. A dangerous place, Burma. I've only ever been there once.
INTERVIEWER: Is there anywhere you haven't been?
RACHEL MARKS: Tasmania. But I'm going there next month. They say it's …

Exercise 10

1 Is it the most interesting place you've been to?
2 I've been to China a number of times.
3 … but I've never written a book about it.
4 I've only ever been there once.
5 Is there anywhere you haven't been?

Unit 18

Exercise 2

1 Can you watch the dog, please?
2 Do you like chips?
3 Can you cash this for me?
4 What would you like? New Shoes.
5 Are those animals sheep?
6 Would you like a cherry?
7 I'm looking for the shops.

Exercise 6

1 This restaurant is quite expensive.
   I think it's really expensive.
2 This wine is quite nice.
   I think it's really nice.
3 These beds are quite comfortable.
   I think they're really comfortable.
4 These magazines are quite interesting.
   I think they're really interesting.
5 This story is quite old.
   I think it's really old.
6 This exercise is quite easy.
   I think it's really easy.

Exercise 7

Once upon a time a princess was lost one night in the snow. She came to a large palace, where there lived a king and his son. She knocked on the door, and the prince answered it. 'Please, let me come in and stay the night,' she said. 'I am a princess and I am lost and it is snowing.'

The prince let her in, and gave her something to eat and let her warm herself by the fire. He went to his father, the king, and said, 'There is a princess who is lost in the snow, and she is very beautiful and I would like to marry her.'

The king said 'How do you know she is a real princess? We have to prove she is a real princess.' 'But how?' said the prince. 'Listen to me,' said the king.

That night, when the princess was tired and ready to sleep, the prince collected one hundred mattresses and piled them one on top of the other. Under the bottom mattress he put a single pea. He took the princess to her room, and said, 'There is your bed'. The princess climbed to the top of the one hundred mattresses and lay down.

The next morning, when the king and the prince were having breakfast, the princess came in. She looked tired and unhappy. 'Did you sleep well?' asked the prince. 'No, I slept very badly,' she said. 'There was something under the mattresses, and I am black and blue. I didn't sleep a wink.'

'It was only a pea', said the king. 'You are indeed a real princess'. And he gave his son permission to marry her, and they lived happily ever after.

Unit 19

Exercise 3

1 I'll cook breakfast.
  I'll cook breakfast.
2 Do you love me?
  Will you love me?
3 I won't go to the party.
  I want to go to the party.
4 I love you.
  I love you.
5 I'll always love you.
  I always love you.
6 We write every day.
  We'll write every day.
7 They won't eat their dinner.
  They won't eat their dinner.

Exercise 5

1 So, you're going to stay in a hotel. What will you do when you arrive?
  I'll unpack my case.
2 Then what will you do?
  I'll have a shower.
3 Then what will you do?
  I'll go for a walk.
4 Then what will you do?
  I'll buy a map.
5 Then what will you do?
  I'll go to a restaurant.
6 Then what will you do?
  I'll watch TV.
7 Then what will you do?
  I'll go to bed.

Exercise 7

A: Have a look at these houses here. What about this one, eh? It's got five bedrooms and a tennis court!
B: We don't need a tennis court. Who plays tennis? Where is it?
A: Near Colchester. Fifty minutes from Liverpool Street Station.
B: Too far. What about this one? It's got six bedrooms and two bathrooms and a double garage.
A: But it costs a quarter of a million! And it's only an attached cottage. Where is Amberley anyway? Look here's a detached family house with five bedrooms. £60,000, that's not too bad.
B: But it's in Dorset, darling.
A: So it is. What about this: easy commuting distance to London.
B: Where is it?
A: It doesn't say. It's a three bedroom cottage, with a garden.
B: Sounds a bit small. How much is it?
A: £125,000. It has a large kitchen.
B: Well, it's a possibility.
A: What do you think? Shall we have a look at it?
B: OK. What's the phone number …

Unit 20

Exercise 2

technology   mathematics
chemistry   arithmetic
biology   university
examinations library
geography   education

Exercise 3

1 Do you want to read in English?
  Yes, reading English is really important.
2 Do you want to write in English?
  Yes, writing in English is really important.
3 Do you want to learn vocabulary?
  Yes, learning vocabulary is really important.
4 Do you want to do grammar exercises?
  Yes, doing grammar exercises is really important.
5 Do you want to be corrected?
  Yes, being corrected is really important.
6 Do you want to communicate fluently?
  Yes, communicating fluently is really important.
7 Do you want to watch films in English?
  Yes, watching films in English is really important

Exercise 6

INTERVIEWER: Alison, what's a typical day at school?
ALISON: Well, I usually get to work at 8.15 and I spend the first hour setting up the classroom. The children come to school at quarter past nine and we spend the first half an hour doing reading. That takes us to quarter to ten and then we'll do some maths work until playtime. Playtime's at quarter to eleven. The children go to the playground for quarter of an hour so they're back in the classroom at eleven o'clock. That gives us an hour and a half until lunch time. I tend to do something practical then; like science or art or practical maths. After lunch, which is at 12.30, they come back to the classroom and I will do some sort of English work then. We might write a story or read some poetry, do some comprehension, that sort of thing. They have another playtime at half past two until quarter to three. At quarter to three we might do some games, some P.E., or some gymnastics and then I spend the last quarter of an hour reading a story. The children go home at 3.45 but I tend to stay on and do some work until about half past five.

Acknowledgements

We are indebted to the following for permission to reproduce copyright material:

The author's agent for adapted extract from *A Book of Middle Eastern Food* by Claudia Roden (Penguin, 1970); Solo Syndication & Literary Agency Ltd for an adapted extract from the article 'It's going to get worse' by Paul Cheston in the *Evening Standard* 8.2.91; Time Out Magazine Limited for an extract from *Time Out* Magazine 12-19 October 1988; the author's agent for an adapted extract from *The Spanish Table* by Marimar Torres (Ebury Press, 1987). Copyright © 1986 by Marimar Torres.

We have unfortunately been unable to trace the copyright holders of the advertisements 'Australia/New Zealand – Round the World' and hotel advertisements in Beijing (Tourist Publications) and would appreciate any information which would enable us to do so.

We are grateful to the following for permission to reproduce photographs and other copyright material:

Associated Press, page 21 left; Barnaby's Picture Library, pages 10 (photo Anne Crabbe) and 12 (photo Norman D. Price); John Birdsall Photography, pages 16 and 17; Camera Press (UK), pages 33, 48 above (photo Werner Braun), 48 above centre (photo R.J.Chinwalla) and 48 below (photo Werner Braun); J. Allan Cash Photolibrary, page 48 below centre; *Daily Telegraph Concise World Atlas*, page 49; Mary Evans Picture Library, page 56 right; Hulton Picture Company, pages 21 right, 56 left and 58; Minerva Books, page 53; Punch Publications, page 36; *Running Magazine*, page 30; University of Reading, page 50; Norman Watson and *Arena Magazine* May/June 1991, page 26. The photograph on page 61 was supplied by the author.

Illustrated by David Bowyer, Ann Johns, Pip Adams, Trevor Stanesby, Philip Bannister, Donald Gott, Kathy Baxendale, Taurus Graphics, Gary Wing and Michael Hill.